THE
BEST TRAIN
JOURNEYS
IN THE WORLD

SHELTER HARBOR PRESS
NEW YORK

Contents

Introduction

I have always loved trains, and as a young man, I was fortunate enough to travel on the last trains to be pulled by steam locomotives. Though it was not permitted then—and rightly so—I can now admit that I have managed to ride in the cab of a steam locomotive more than once. The memory of these journeys, alongside the train drivers amid the coal, smoke, and steam, still thrills me today. So, for me, traveling either for work or pleasure means to hop on a train. In this volume, we have brought together forty journeys from around the globe whose fascination and enjoyment are only enhanced when traveling on a train. When you think about it, there is no better way to travel: there is no need to drive, there are none of the space and luggage restrictions found in air travel, and on a train, passengers arrive in the heart of the city, having discovered new territories from their windows. They have walked alongside the coaches, had a coffee or lunch in the dining car, and met interesting people, perhaps new friends—or even new loves.

The itineraries we have selected differ from each other significantly, not just because their locations range from the Australian desert to the Arctic Circle, but also because they provide examples of different ways one can travel by train. Some of these trains provide public transportation services to their region each day, offering a way to be immersed in the daily life of a place and to understand its customs and curiosities. Others are exclusive tourist trains—true five-star hotels on rails—like the legendary Orient Express. On these trains, in addition to enjoying an extremely high level of service, a passenger can imagine what it must have been like to travel on a luxury train in the late nineteenth century or early decades of the twentieth. These trips can last up to fifteen days, with stops in numerous locations to explore cities and sites of particular interest. On other tourist trains, the journey lasts only a few hours or a couple of days at the most. Comfort is essential, but the main attraction is the landscape traveled.

In short, a train is a method of travel suited to everyone. One can spend very little to do so, by taking advantage of the Interrail Pass, for example. On the other hand, passengers can also spend a small fortune in the case of certain long luxury journeys, which can be matched perfectly with their interests. Those who are passionate about railroad history and technology will find historic trains pulled by steam locomotives or true relics of a bygone era, like La Trochita in Argentine Patagonia or the Toy Train in the Himalayan mountains of India. Hiking enthusiasts may choose the Aurora Winter Train in Alaska, and those wishing to experience a tropical rainforest adventure can get on Madagascar's Fianarantsoa–Côte Est line, for which one can be certain of the time and day of departure, but not of arrival.

For each of these train journeys, we have sought to provide key information, such as the distance and

duration of each journey, suggestions for potential stopovers, and a brief summary of the historical and economic reasoning that led to a railroad line's construction or the establishment of a particular train. Featuring an array of illustrations, this text will also describe each journey's itinerary, various stops, and other key points of interest, as well as the different qualities of each train. There are also suggestions concerning what levels of service to choose on board whenever available. Finally, a small description can be found with useful practical information for travelers. Rather than a traditional travel manual, this volume is a story told through images, describing the timeless fascination the railroad still holds all around the globe. It is also an invitation to break through any hesitation, put yourself out there, and come aboard one of these trains, perhaps starting with the line closest to home. You will not be disappointed.

Aurora Winter Train

Among the dogsleds, beneath the Northern Lights…
Alaska dressed for winter.

Crossing Alaska in winter by train is, without a doubt, an intense, captivating experience. It conjures images from the movie *Runaway Train*, in which two convicts at large find themselves escaping on a freight train without a driver, making a mad dash through freezing, snow-covered Alaskan forests. A ride aboard the **Aurora Winter Train** between Anchorage and Fairbanks is, of course, nothing so dramatic, but it is certainly a marvelous adventure not easily forgotten. This train, halfway between a tourist train and an ordinary passenger train serving the (sparse) population living between the cities at each end of the route, is operated by the Alaska Railroad and runs along the 760-kilometer-long (472-mile-long) single, standard-gauge track uniting the two major Alaskan municipalities. The route, to be precise, begins 183 kilometers (114 miles) south of Anchorage, in the city of Seward. The line, which took twenty years to construct, was inaugurated in 1923, and in 1985, its ownership was transferred from the federal government to the Alaskan government.

The railroad is an important one, especially for connecting more isolated inland areas and, of course, for tourism. The service is certainly not a crowded experience, however, given that the passenger average in 2021 was no greater than one hundred people per day.

One of the railroad's unique train services is the Hurricane Turn, a train that ensures a connection for those living between the towns of Talkeetna and Hurricane. This area is still lacking in roads, and the railroad is the only form of transportation residents have for traveling to other towns for food and supplies. Travelers can board the Hurricane Turn at any point along its route by simply holding up a large white flag or a light piece of cloth (the reason it is called a **"flagstop" service**). The Aurora Winter Train, which runs during the hard winter months,

Departure: Anchorage
Arrival: Fairbanks
Distance: 760 km (472 miles)
Duration: 12 hours
Stages: 2
Country: USA – Alaska

6 – An image of the Aurora Winter Train in evening headed to Fairbanks conveying the sense of adventure felt on this journey.

7 – A magnificent view of the Northern Lights setting the night sky alight in Fairbanks. This display alone is worth the entire trip through the Alaskan cold.

Fairbanks

Healy

Denali

Hurricane

Talkeetna

Wasilia

Anchorage

Seward

*8 – The frosty morning light illuminates the Aurora Winter Train as it crosses a
stream, with fogbanks gently rising from it.*

9 – Dogsledding is one Alaskan experience that cannot be missed.

offers this service to the local area as well. This feature of the railway
offers a good glimpse of both the territory being crossed and the
train's important role, guaranteeing its run throughout the year. The
Aurora Winter Train has a regular weekend schedule from September
15 to May 15, departing from Anchorage on Saturday morning and
arriving around twelve hours later in Fairbanks. The next day, Sunday,
the train travels the line in reverse, in the same time. Some midweek
departures are also available.

Passengers can choose between simply booking a train ticket
or opting for an Alaska Railroad adventure package. These are
multiday itineraries that include rail travel, accommodation, and local
activities for a comprehensive, hassle-free **Alaska adventure**. Winter
packages range from just a weekend to a five-night exploration of
the country's far north. And, speaking of nighttime, one of the most
fascinating opportunities offered by a winter tour on this train is
a chance to admire the Northern Lights while in Fairbanks. These
tours, organized collaboratively by Alaska Railroad and local tour

operators, allow guests to enjoy experiences the region is known for, such as dogsledding, to discover the most interesting local spots, and to take part in sporting activities, especially cross-country skiing and snowshoe treks. The Saturday-Sunday Aurora Winter Train schedule from Anchorage, for example, is perfect for a weekend in Talkeetna. From there, guests can explore the area's network of winter trails on skis.

The most popular all-inclusive package allows travelers to make their own way to Anchorage ready to take the the Aurora Winter Train on Tuesday morning at 8:30 a.m., admiring Mount Denali and the landscape of Denali National Park from the window as they head north toward Talkeetna. The stopover in this small town can be extended on Wednesdays with a long excursion on dogsleds and dinner in the evening at a local restaurant in downtown Talkeetna. Travelers board the train again on Thursday, skirting the national park and crossing the Alaska Range on the journey. In the evening, the train arrives in Fairbanks, where passengers will remain Friday and Saturday, spending their time hiking and sightseeing during the day, then viewing the **Northern Lights** viewing from evening late into the night. The weekday Aurora Winter train is effectively just a tourist train, stopping only at regular stations..

This tourist package is also available for the reverse north-south route, and it can include flights arriving in Anchorage and departing from Fairbanks.

On the regular Aurora Winter Train, running on Saturdays and Sundays, travelers can create their own itinerary to include stops and excursions, but it must be kept in mind that tickes are not flexible. In other words, if a ticket is purchased from Anchorage to Fairbanks, the passenger holding the ticket will not be able to exit an intermediate station and then continue with that same ticket to their destination on the next day's train. Two tickets must be purchased for each of the two legs and for the exact day of intended travel. Travelers who are adventurous and well-equipped can make use of the flagstop service as local passengers do, getting off and on, more or less in the middle of nowhere.

If the cold is too biting, and one is not experienced enough to hike in such harsh environments, enjoyment of the Alaskan winter landscape from the comfort of a cozy train carriage, complete with large picture windows and onboard dining, is still recommended. Alaska Railway trains offer two classes of service: the GoldStar Service—which, however, is only available on the Coastal Classic

In summertime, the Denali Star train leaves Anchorage every day for a twelve-hour journey north to Fairbanks, while a sister train in Fairbanks makes the same journey in the other direction. Along the way, the Denali Star stops at Wasilla, Talkeetna, and Denali National Park. On clear days, passengers enjoy spectacular views of the mountain the train is named after: Denali, the highest peak in North America. It is the ideal train to reach Denali National Park. A trip to the park in the summertime immerses visitors in a still-wild, unspoiled natural world—the true soul of Alaska. Adventure Class and GoldStar Service are available on board.

and Denali Star trains, both operating only in the summertime—and Adventure Class, available on all trains. Restaurant and bar service is available on all Alaska Railroad routes, except for the Hurricane Turn. Keep in mind that no Alaska Railroad trains accept cash, and onboard purchases must be made by credit or debit card.

Winter in Alaska is not for everyone, but those with enough of a feeling for adventure discover a true wonderland, enrobed in a winter mantle. Thick blankets of snow add to the fascination of these unspoiled landscapes, and the long, dark nights set the perfect stage for the Aurora Borealis to mysteriously appear.

CANADA
BANFF TO VANCOUVER

Departure: Banff
Arrival: Vancouver
Distance: 956 km (594 miles)
Duration: 2 days
Stages: 1
Country: Canada

10/11 – The Rocky Mountaineer meanders along its tracks in the Cheakamus River valley in the Rocky Mountains.

11 top – The panoramic coach provided for the travelers choosing GoldLeaf Service aboard the Rocky Mountaineer.

11 bottom – The Rocky Mountaineer is pulled by two diesel locomotives on the most demanding stretches of track, the first locomotive displaying the train's logo in front.

Rocky Mountaineer

Chasing the First Passage to the West and the legendary gold rush on an elegant luxury train amid the Canadian Rockies.

The **Rocky Mountaineer** is a luxury train operated by the private company Rocky Mountaineer Vacations. It is considered one of the best in the world for the experience it provides its passengers, thanks to four different itineraries traversing the spectacular scenery of the Canadian Rockies. Tourists can purchase tour packages that include activities in the cities of departure or arrival, or just buy one-way or round trip tickets for the four routes: Vancouver–Kamloops–Banff, a route dubbed the First Passage to the West; Vancouver–Kamloops–Jasper, or the Journey through the Clouds; Vancouver–Whistler–Quesnel–Jasper, which travels under the name of Rainforest to Goldrush; and Circle Journeys, which depart and arrive in Vancouver. All four journeys are beautiful, and it is a challenge to select one if there is no personal preference for one of the specific areas traversed.

All Rocky Mountaineer journeys last between two and three days, but unlike most other luxury tourist trains, they do not involve spending the night aboard the train. The Rocky Mountaineer travels only during the day, allowing passengers to enjoy the spectacular landscapes traveled. They then spend the night in a five-star hotel in one of the cities with the price included in their ticket. This choice also aims to simplify the logistics and organization of the train itself, bypassing everything concerning overnight passenger accommodations.

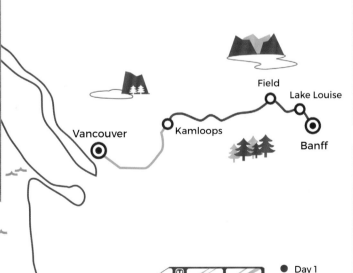

Field
Lake Louise

Vancouver
Kamloops
Banff

● Day 1
● Day 2

PRACTICAL TIPS

THE FREQUENCY OF THE ROCKY MOUNTAINEER
FIRST PASSAGE TO THE WEST ROUTE, LIKE THE OTHER
ITINERARIES, IS SUBJECT TO CHANGE, SO CHECKING THE
ACTUAL TRAVEL DATES IN ADVANCE IS ADVISED.

USEFUL WEBSITES
Rocky Mountaineer:
https://www.rockymountaineer.com

12 – Banff National Park, which surrounds the Rocky Mountaineer's departure city, is home to enchanting spots like Moraine Lake.

13 top – The train passes through parts of the Rocky Mountains with some of the most beautiful views in all of Canada.

It follows, then, that there are no sleeping cars in the train's design, and its entire structure is devoted to allowing travelers not to miss even a minute of the magnificent landscape outside the train. All of its carriages are panoramic, but some are more so than others. There are in fact two classes of service offered: SilverLeaf and GoldLeaf. Both allow passengers to fully enjoy views of the Rocky Mountains, and the choice must be made according to the expense one is willing to take on and the level of service desired. The view is better in the bilevel GoldLeaf coaches since they are higher off the ground. Breakfast and lunch are also served in a dining car and not at one's seat. Last, but not least, with this ticket, passengers can access the **open viewing platform** at the back of the train, where they can take photos and videos without window reflections.

All itineraries offered on the Rocky Mountaineer are charming, but this chapter will focus on the Vancouver–Kamloops–Banff route, the First Passage to the West. This route was selected, since it follows the Canadian Pacific Railway, Canada's first transcontinental line, inaugurated in 1885. It was also the first route traveled by the Rocky Mountaineer, in 1990. Moreover, while it is a tourist train, it is the only passenger train that travels this historic Canadian line today.

The Rocky Mountaineer makes this route several times a week in both directions from April to October. It lasts two full days and includes a night in a hotel at Kamloops.

There is really no difference concerning the quality of the trip in terms of views and services on board when traveling east to west or vice versa. But, it would be more in keeping with the spirit of the pioneers who first took the railroad westward, to depart from Banff. This small tourist town of less than 8,000 inhabitants is over 1,400 meters (4,500 feet) above sea level, and is the most important town located in the national park that bears its name. The park extends over 6,500 square kilometers (2,500 square miles) and hosts a population of wild animals, including grizzly bears and moose, that is certainly greater than the number of people living in Banff. The best way to get there is a flight to Calgary, 104 kilometers (65 miles) away, and then by car or via one of the bus lines that connect the city to the airport.

The Rocky Mountaineer awaits passengers early in the morning at Banff station, just outside the city center. The building dates back to 1910, when it took the place of the shed that originally marked a stopping point for the first trains running on the line from 1885.

From the journey's very first miles, the landscape is magnificent in every direction. Then, after half an hour, the massive, isolated form of Castle Mountain makes its appearance. A few miles on, the train makes a wide curve: this is now known as the **Morant's Curve**, named after Nicholas Morant, a photographer for the Canadian Pacific Railway, who immortalized it in dozens of images that have appeared in books all over the globe.

After this iconic site, the train passes the Lake Louise station, which was built entirely of wood in 1909 and was declared a heritage railway station by Canada's federal government in 1991.

A few miles on, a monument along the platform to the left of the train marks another significant place in the journey: the Continental Divide, the hydrological divide between the Atlantic and Pacific Oceans, and the highest point of the entire route, with an elevation of 1,625 meters (just over 5,330 feet). The line continues on, taking curves, bridges, and tunnels through an inaccessible, wild territory that posed a true challenge when the tracks were originally laid.

This becomes clear continuing along the route, when the train enters the first of the two spiral tunnels that allow the train to descend rapidly without an excessive slope.

After the tunnels, the train stops at the Field station, then enters

13 center – In an area with no roads, a view of the Rocky Mountaineer from a plane: the only way people can see it traveling through this forest in the Rockies.

13 bottom – The Rocky Mountaineer passes the unmistakable silhouette of Mount Rundle along the bank of the Vermilion Lakes in Banff.

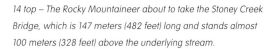

14 top – The Rocky Mountaineer about to take the Stoney Creek Bridge, which is 147 meters (482 feet) long and stands almost 100 meters (328 feet) above the underlying stream.

14 bottom – Another of the famous bridges on the rail line between Banff and Vancouver, this one over the Fraser River in Lillooet, British Columbia.

14/15 – The Rocky Mountaineer runs along Seton Lake: here, the railroad managed to find a seemingly impossible strip of land between the lake and the rock face.

Kicking Horse Canyon, a name once given to this railroad route through the Rocky Mountains. Here, the track follows the river for several miles, with many bridges and numerous tunnels. Traveling another two hours or so, the Rocky Mountaineer crosses the famous **Stoney Creek Bridge**, which is 147 meters (482 feet) long and rises 100 meters (328 feet) over the stream below. Today, this section of the route can be bypassed via a tunnel built to increase the line's capacity, but the Rocky Mountaineer has rightly chosen to follow the original route precisely because of this structure, as well as two smaller, but equally spectacular bridges. The train arrives in Kamloops in the evening for the overnight stop.

The next day, the train runs along the edge of Kamloops Lake, then follows the Thompson River through an unusually arid landscape to its confluence with the Fraser River. Along one side of the entire valley's edge are tracks from the Canadian Pacific, a line built in 1885, while those of the Canadian National, built in 1917, run along the other. The train finally exits the Fraser River Canyon for what becomes a flat landscape on its approach to Vancouver in the evening, the Rocky Mountains now behind the passengers.

INTERESTING FACTS

The Canadian Pacific Railway's spiral consists of two tunnels that curve approximately 270 degrees along the sides of the valley. The higher tunnel, "number one," is nearly 910 meters (3,000 feet) long and runs underneath Cathedral Mountain. The track exits the tunnel in the opposite direction, 15 meters (50 feet) beneath the track where it entered. It then continues along the edge of the valley in the opposite direction of its previous route before crossing the Kicking Horse River and entering Mount Ogden. This tunnel, "number two," also curves 270 degrees, and its exit is, again, about 15 meters (50 feet) below its entrance. From here, the line continues down to the valley in its original direction, toward Field. Its construction and additional track effectively double the length of the route, reducing the line's slope to 2.2%, as opposed to the original 4.5%.

CANADA
TORONTO TO VANCOUVER

Departure: Toronto
Arrival: Vancouver
Distance: 4,466 km (2,775 miles)
Duration: 4 days
Stages: 1
Country: Canada

16/17 – The Canadian, with its panoramic coaches, crosses the Canadian Rockies, with Mount Robson behind, standing 3,954 meters (nearly 13,000 feet) high.

The Canadian

Discovering Canada between Toronto and Vancouver, on the longest railway service in North America.

If you would simply like to travel from Toronto to Vancouver, there are much faster means of transportation than the train—the average duration of a flight between Canada's two major cities is five hours and fifteen minutes. However, if you would like to see what truly lies in Canada between Toronto and Vancouver, then hop aboard the **Canadian** and enjoy the four-day, four-night ride on the longest passenger rail service in North America.

Departing from Toronto, the train makes its way through the crowded urban area then crosses the Great Lakes region of Ontario and continues to run its journey through the vast, rugged, generally sparsley populated territory of the Canadian Shield, characterized by rocky outcrops alternating with forests and wetland areas. It weaves through the Rocky Mountains, then cuts through the rocky Fraser Valley in the province of British Columbia before finally arriving, after 4,466 kilometers (2,775 miles), on the Pacific coast in the sparkling city of Vancouver. It is therefore no coincidence that every year thousands of travelers from all over the world, including many Canadians, decide to undertake one of the most beautiful journeys by train in the Northern Hemisphere.

The history of the transcontinental railway that connects the eastern side of the country to the Pacific side is intertwined with Canada's own history. In 1880, the Canadian government entrusted the task of building the first

17 – The train crosses one of the trestle bridges spanning the numerous waterways in the Canadian Rocky Mountain region.

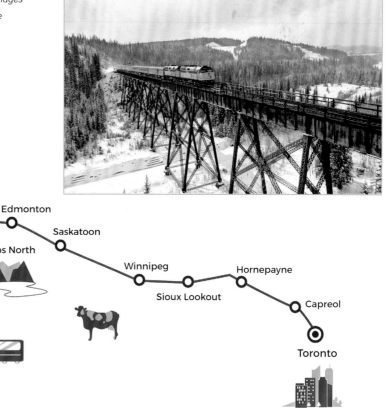

PRACTICAL TIPS

THE CANADIAN TRANSCONTINENTAL TRAIN TRAVELS TWICE A WEEK ALL YEAR ROUND AND IS OPERATED BY VIA RAIL CANADA, THE CANADIAN NATIONAL RAIL OPERATOR. TICKETS CAN BE PURCHASED ONLINE ON THE COMPANY'S WEBSITE, FOR THE ENTIRE ROUTE OR FOR ANY OTHER STRETCH BETWEEN TWO STATIONS ON THE LINE. THERE ARE NO PARTICULAR DIFFERENCES IN TRAVEL FROM EAST TO WEST OR VICE VERSA, EXCEPT FOR SOME AREAS THAT MAY BE CROSSED IN THE DARK. IN ANY CASE, THE TRAIN IS ALMOST ALWAYS DELAYED BY A FEW HOURS DUE TO TRAFFIC, AND IT IS DIFFICULT TO BE SURE OF THE TRANSIT TIMES AT THE MOST SCENIC STOPS. VIA RAIL THEREFORE RECOMMENDS THAT TRAVELERS DO NOT BOOK TRAVEL CONNECTIONS THAT ARE TOO CLOSE TO THE TRAIN'S SCHEDULED ARRIVAL TIME.

USEFUL WEBSITES
VIA Rail Canada: **https://www.viarail.ca**

Jasper National Park: **https://www.pc.gc.ca/en/pn-np/ab/jasper**

18 – The Canadian travels through some of the most beautiful and unspoiled Canadian regions, which can be easily admired inside its panoramic cars.

19 top – The historic Union Station in Toronto where the train departs for Vancouver, with the CN Tower in the background standing 553 meters (about 1,815 feet) high.

19 bottom – Autumn in Winnipeg, one of the cities on the Canadian's itinerary, is known for its bright and vivid colors.

line connecting east and west coasts to the Canadian Pacific Railway. Over the next five years, the railway company laid over 4,600 kilometers (2,850 miles) of track while also connecting the country's shorter lines that had already been built. It was a huge operation, completed in record time (six years earlier than expected), stimulating growth in the vast western areas' population and development. One need only recall that most of western Canada's large cities were founded and grew around the stations of the Canadian Pacific Railway. Taking this trip today is like walking through the history of Canada itself.

The Canadian is made up of original Canadian and American cars from the 1950s, which have been completely refurbished while keeping to the era's unmistakable style. In the summer months (as the train runs all year round), it comprises over twenty cars, and even if most travelers are tourists, the task of the train today is still to ensure a connection to the remote locations between Capreol and Winnipeg, making many stops at small stations on the line.

All coaches, housed in distinctive stainless steel, have large windows. Some, however, dubbed "Skyline" cars, feature a top-floor **panoramic observation dome**. Seats inside the dome are, of course, highly coveted. The bar is located in the central area beneath the observation dome, serving drinks and microwave-prepared hot meals. This is not the only onboard catering service, as the train also has a dining car (two in summertime) reserved for passengers who book a space in the sleeping cars. A special car is attached to the rear of the train: the Park car, the Canadian's emblematic vehicle. In 1954–55, the Canadian Pacific Railway created eighteen Park cars, all named after famous Canadian national parks. The Park car features a Bullet Lounge at the rear, offering exceptional views of the tracks, and an observation dome on the upper level with a full-service bar with tables and chairs beneath it.

The other carriages in the train's arrangement offer passengers various levels of service: one can travel in Economy class in a comfortable reclining seat, or book something more expensive, up to the much more welcoming service provided in its Sleeper Plus class, which offers an exclusive sleeping compartment and includes all dining car meals in the ticket price. Between these two ends of the spectrum, a very popular solution is a cabin with a couch that turns into a comfortable single bed at night.

There are various options for sleeping arrangements (single or double), which progress up to the most luxurious, exclusive option of the previously mentioned Sleeper Plus class and, for some

years now, Prestige class, which includes five-star hotel service and fixtures. The trip is therefore within everyone's reach, from the penniless globetrotting young backpacker to the more affluent tourist with traditional tastes who is not looking to sacrifice any comfort.

The areas served by the Canadian over the nearly 4,500 kilometers (2,800 miles) of its route are many, but the main stops are Capreol, Sioux Lookout, Winnipeg, Saskatoon, Edmonton, Jasper, and the Kamloops North station.

The journey begins in the morning in the monumental, crowded Toronto Union Station, surrounded by ultramodern skyscrapers and overlooked by the 553 meters (1,815 feet) of the CN Tower, one of the tallest telecommunications towers in the world. Departing the sprawling Canadian metropolis, the landscape quickly changes, and the Canadian starts across the great Canadian Shield among lakes, rivers separated by woods, and outcrops of ancient rock.

This region extends nearly to Winnipeg and is very sparsely

From Jasper station, the Canadian allows travelers to easily reach Jasper National Park, the largest and wildest in Canada. Its territory extends over a vast region of rugged trails and mountainous terrain, contrasted with fragile, protected ecosystems like the world-famous Columbia Icefield, which in the last 125 years has receded by nearly a mile. The park is also rich in wildlife and is home to some of North America's most significant populations of grizzly bears, elk, and moose, in addition to thousands of plant and insect species. There are more than 900 kilometers (550 miles) of hiking trails to explore there, bearing in mind that visitors should disturb the animals and the natural balance as little as possible. Due to the incredible wildlife populating it, the park has been designated a UNESCO World Heritage Site.

inhabited, in contrast to the high urban density of Toronto. The train arrives in Winnipeg in the evening. on the second day, after having traveled over 1,943 kilometers (1,200 miles). It stops there for two hours, in part to allow for refueling of the diesel locomotives and to change staff. This city, capital of the province of Manitoba, is located on the eastern edge of the Canadian Prairies region. It is an important railroad and highway hub, and for this reason it is called the "Gateway to the West."

From here, the Canadian begins to cross endless prairies dotted with farms and grazing animals. In Saskatoon, the train stops for about half an hour before resuming its journey and crossing the famed **Fabyan Trestle Bridge**, built in 1909, 845 meters (2,775 feet) long and 59 meters (195 feet) high, on the Battle River nearly halfway to Edmonton. The train arrives in Edmonton at around 9:00 p.m. on the third day of travel, stopping until midnight. The Canadian, whose identification number is 1 when on schedule, aims to depart Alberta's capital exactly one minute after midnight, beginning its fourth day of travel and arriving in the morning. in

Jasper, where it stops for three hours.

On this stretch, the route crosses the **Rocky Mountains**, illuminated by the sun rising behind the train. It is one of the most spectacular parts of the journey, and it can also be enjoyed by passengers who are not early-risers since, after about 3,600 kilometers (2,200 miles), the train is practically always running a few hours behind the scheduled time. The delay, providential in this case, is due to the single track, which forces numerous stops to allow the very long Canadian freight trains, the true masters of this line, to cross.

The journey nears its end: after Kamloops North, where the train stops on the evening of the fourth day and is refueled, the track runs along Kamloops Lake and then enters the bare, rocky gorge of the Fraser River.

In the morning of the fifth day, the Canadian finally enters Vancouver's historic Pacific Central Station, built in 1919, where visitors can take a taxi or bus to reach the center of the grand and beautiful capital of the Canadian West.

20 top – The Walterdale Bridge over the North Saskatchewan River in Edmonton. Built in 2017, it replaced the old bridge which dated back to 1913.

20 center – A glimpse of the landscape around the Canadian Rockies from sides of the Canadian.

20 bottom – The Athabasca River in the Rocky Mountains' Jasper National Park, the largest in Canada. In the background, the mountain massif of Whistlers Peak.

20/21 – The Canadian's long line of coaches moves along the banks of Moose Lake in Jasper National Park.

USA

CHICAGO TO SEATTLE OR PORTLAND

Departure: Chicago
Arrival: Seattle or Portland
Distance: 3,550 km (2,206 miles) Seattle / 3,632 km (2,257 miles) Portland
Duration: 46 hours
Stages: 3
Country: USA – Illinois, Wisconsin, Minnesota, North Dakota, Montana, Ida
Washington, and Oregon

22/23 – Along the north bank of the Columbia River, the Portland set of the Empire Builder approaches the Wishram stop, just beyond Tunnel 12.

Empire Builder

From Chicago to the Pacific coast, following the route many Americans took seeking their fortune out west at the end of the nineteenth century.

A trip with the **Empire Builder**, Amtrak's long-distance train that takes passengers from Chicago to the Pacific coast—either to Seattle, Washington, or Portland, Oregon, according to preference—allows them to discover the Northwest's incomparable landscapes and directly access Montana's Glacier National Park via specially dedicated stations.

Without stopping, the journey lasts two days—forty-six hours, to be precise—and crosses eight states: Illinois, Wisconsin, Minnesota, North Dakota, Montana, Idaho, Washington, and Oregon. Of course, passengers can choose to organize a one-night or longer stay at one of the stops. The service runs daily in both directions, which allows passengers to easily resume their journey the day after making a stop.

The schedule is set for the train to cross the Rocky Mountains and stop at Glacier National Park stations during the day, whether traveling from Chicago toward the Pacific or the reverse. Starting from the Pacific coast,

23 – The Chicago skyline at sunrise.

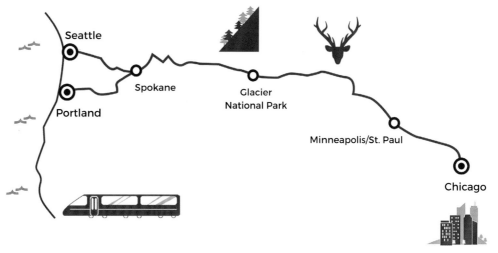

PRACTICAL TIPS

IF TIME ALLOWS, IT COULD BE A GOOD IDEA TO BREAK UP THE ROUTE BY STOPPING FOR A DAY IN ONE OR MORE OF THE CITIES ON THE LINE BEFORE RESUMING THE JOURNEY. TO MAKE THESE INTERMEDIATE STOPS, ONE NEEDS TO BUY SEPARATE TICKETS FOR EACH LEG. TO BOOK A TRIP WITH STOPOVERS IN ALL THE DESIRED CITIES, JUST LOOK FOR THE "MULTI-CITY" LINK IN THE TOP LEFT CORNER OF THE BOOKING FORM ON AMTRAK'S WEBSITE, OR CLICK "ADD TRIP" BELOW THE TRAVEL INFORMATION FIELDS. THIS ALLOWS PASSENGERS TO BOOK A TRIP WITH UP TO FOUR LEGS. OF COURSE, ADDITIONAL LEGS CAN BE BOOKED SEPARATELY.

USEFUL WEBSITES
Amtrak: **https://www.amtrak.com**

especially in winter, one does have a few more hours of light to enjoy the most spectacular part of the track. The route from Chicago is 3,632 kilometers (2,257 miles) long to Portland and 3,550 kilometers (2,206 miles) to Seattle. At the Spokane station, the train from Chicago divides into two sections, one going to Seattle and the other to Portland. The opposite happens, of course, going in the opposite direction.

The Empire Builder was established by the Great Northern Railway in 1929 and quickly became the railway company's most iconic train. Air transport was underdeveloped at the time, and the train was the only means of transport connecting U.S. cities. The name of the train is a tribute to James J. Hill, who had been nicknamed "the Empire Builder." Hill was the man who made the Great Northern Railway "great," laying tracks to the Pacific coast at the end of the nineteenth century.

Over the decades, this line saw various adjustments to its route and improvements to rolling stock, including the introduction of

streamlined trains (very in vogue in the early postwar U.S.) with **clear-domed carriages** and a fully panoramic coach for first-class passengers. From that time on, the Empire Builder has thus had a dual personality, as both a means of connection between cities in the northwestern states as well as a train designed for people traveling only for pleasure, somehow anticipating a boom in mass tourism.

The train was first transferred from the Great Northern Railway to Burlington Northern in 1970, and then to Amtrak when the federal company took over all domestic long-distance traffic in 1971.

Like all Amtrak trains, this one is made up of **bilevel Superliner carriages**. At the front are two or three diesel locomotives (their model either a GE Genesis PE42 or Siemens Charger ALC-42), followed by a Viewliner baggage car, a crew car providing a connection to the subsequent bilevel cars, two sleeping cars, a restaurant, two cars with reclining seats, and a lounge/café car with panoramic views. These cars all make up the section taking the route to Seattle from Spokane. The rear of the train, routed to Portland, includes a car with reclining seats (partially occupied by a baggage area), a second car with seats, a sleeper car, and an additional car with seating, limited to the stretch between Chicago and St. Paul, Minnesota. Much like other Amtrak trains, passengers may book a large reclining seat or a sleeper cabin in various configurations, ranging from the smallest two-seater, called a "Roomette," up to the four-seater cabin for families with children up to the age of twelve.

Let's follow the Empire Builder departing from Chicago, mentally retracing the journey many Americans made seeking their fortune out west. The train leaves Union Station in the mid afternoon, crossing the great, vibrant Illinois metropolis and the vast urban area surrounding it, heading north toward Milwaukee. The urban landscape soon gives way to the pleasant Wisconsin countryside. Crossing the Mississippi River a couple of times, the train reaches St. Paul in the late evening. It stops there for about twenty minutes so the end seating car can be detached from the end of the train.

The train travels across Minnesota overnight, and in the early morning, it heads deep into the state of North Dakota. The Great Plains float by the train windows, with wild animals like coyotes and deer sometimes appearing, as well as towns with largely agricultural economies. Wolf Point is the first station in Montana, where the Empire Builder makes a brief stop soon after midday on the second day of travel. Today, the town has a few thousand

24 – The Empire Builder traverses some of the most beautiful, forested areas of the Rocky Mountains.

25 top – The Empire Builder offers excellent dining service: here, a Superliner coach is set to welcome travelers.

25 bottom – The Empire Builder, pulled by a locomotive in fiftieth-anniversary livery, crosses the North Fork Skykomish River at Index.

For much of the line, the Empire Builder follows the westward route opened by the Lewis and Clark Expedition between 1804 and 1806. Promoted by President Thomas Jefferson, that expedition's mission was to explore and map the Louisiana Territory, which had just been acquired from the French via treaty (roughly corresponding to the area of all today's central U.S. states, from the northernmost part of Texas to the Canadian border), and to trace a route through the western half of the continent. Jefferson intended to establish an American presence in this territory before European powers made claims in the region. Lewis and Clark were also charged with studying plant and animal life, exploring the geography of the area, and establishing trade with local Native American tribes. It was a significant event in the history of the United States.

inhabitants. It is located directly along the route of the **Lewis and Clark** military expedition, which crossed the northwestern region of the United States to the Pacific in 1804 and is considered one of the most significant chapters in American exploration.

This section also passes through the Fort Peck Indian Reservation, one of several Native American reservations along the railroad track.

The landscape remains that of the Northern Plains for a few more hours until, toward sunset, passengers arrive in Glacier National Park, one of the most beautiful in the United States. The Park has 26 glaciers, over 200 lakes, nearly 2,500 kilometers (1,600 miles) of streams, impressive waterfalls, and majestic mountain peaks. Here the train stops at Browning, East Glacier Park, Essex, and West Glacier Park, all of which give easy access to the Park (though some stops are only seasonal). Due to specially designed local bus services, passengers need not rent a car when alighting at these stations to visit the park or go skiing in wintertime.

26 – The Empire Builder stops at four stations where passengers can embark on a hike in Glacier National Park. In the photo: a glimpse of Lake Josephine.

27 top – The Logan Pass Trail in Glacier National Park on a sunny day.

27 bottom – A hike along one of the many streams that cut through Glacier National Park.

The train makes its way across the Rocky Mountains over the second night of travel but makes an important stop in Spokane, where it divides into two sections, one destined for Seattle, one for Portland.

The first follows a more northerly route, crossing the Cascade Mountains and Skykomish River Valley to Puget Sound, the complex, roughly 160-kilometer-deep (100-mile-deep) inlet with Seattle lying on its coast. After about an hour of traveling along the coast, the Empire Builder enters Seattle's King Street Station at around late morning.

The section heading to Portland, meanwhile, travels along the northern bank of the Columbia River Gorge, which is very windy

28/29 – The Seattle skyline with Mount Rainier in the background—the city is one of the Empire Builder's two destinations on the Pacific coast.

28 – The Empire Builder's two sections separate in the city of Spokane: one is bound for Seattle, the other for Portland. Pictured here is autumn in Spokane's Riverfront Park.

29 – A view from above of Union Station, where the Portland section of the Empire Builder concludes its journey.

and popular with surfers. Its banks are marked by surprising dots of yellow wormwood and mugwort flowers. Finally, in the late morning on the third day of travel, the Empire Builder enters Portland's Union Station.

California Zephyr

Travel across the Rocky Mountains and the Nevada desert to the West aboard a legendary train from Chicago to San Francisco.

The **California Zephyr** is still in all probability the most famous and fascinating train in North America. Its route not only crosses some of the most beautiful and exciting parts of the United States but also recalls the American saga of westward expansion. An experience aboard the California Zephyr reminds us that a journey is an opportunity to travel through and discover unknown places and to meet new people, maintaining a sense of constant surprise and wonder that we do not get from airline travel.

This legendary train runs between Chicago and San Francisco, crosses the plains of Iowa, ascends to Denver and climbs the Rocky Mountains to Winter Park, then makes its way into the Nevada desert to stop in Reno, moves up the mountains of the Sierra Nevada, and finally descends in Sacramento before reaching Emeryville station on the outskirts of San Francisco.

An interesting history lies behind the California Zephyr. The thought of making an easy connection to other states in the Union was born in San Francisco in 1939, during the Golden Gate International Exposition. The "Exposition Flyer" train was placed on the rails with promoters intending it to provide a temporary service to Chicago. Yet the success and popularity of the direct link convinced the railway companies to turn it into a regular service with high-quality rolling stock, dubbed the California Zephyr. The first run of the new train, which aimed to distinguish itself from any other long-distance train, took place in 1949.

To offer an idea of the special service on board that made a ride on the California Zephyr truly unique,

30 – A vintage poster designed by Bern Hill for General Motors' Electro-Motive Division promotes the California Zephyr's panoramic "vista dome" coaches.

30/31 – On its journey from Chicago to San Francisco, the California Zephyr climbs the Rockies and the mountains of the Sierra Nevada, traveling through spectacular landscapes.

Departure: Chicago
Arrival: San Francisco
Distance: 3,924 km (2,438 miles)
Duration: 52 hours
Stages: 1 (or more, depending on the time available)
Country: USA – Illinois, Iowa, Nebraska, Colorado, Utah, Nevada, and California

PRACTICAL TIPS

THE ITINERARY CAN BE DIVIDED INTO VARIOUS STAGES, DEDICATING A DAY OR MORE TO EXPLORING THE CITIES LYING ON THE TRAIN'S ROUTE AT ONE'S OWN PACE BEFORE RESUMING THE JOURNEY TOWARD ITS FINAL DESTINATION. IT IS NOT POSSIBLE TO MAKE THESE INTERMEDIATE STOPS WITH A SINGLE TICKET, SO SEPARATE TICKETS MUST BE PURCHASED FOR EACH STRETCH. THIS CAN BE EASILY DONE VIA A LINK WITH THE HEADING OF "MULTI-CITY" AT THE TOP LEFT OF THE ONLINE BOOKING FORM AT WWW .AMTRAK.COM, OR SIMPLY CLICK "ADD TRIP" BELOW THE FIELD FOR DEPARTURE DETAILS. THE SITE ALLOWS FOR A MAXIMUM OF FOUR LEGS AT A TIME, BUT EVEN MORE CAN BE BOOKED BY PURCHASING SEPARATE TICKETS.

USEFUL WEBSITES
Amtrak: **https://www.amtrak.com**

32 – Chicago Union Station, where the westbound California Zephyr departs in the early afternoon.

33 – A panoramic coach on the California Zephyr with seats that swivel in the direction of its large windows, providing panoramic views of the landscape.

just imagine the celebrated **"Zephyrettes,"** hostesses entrusted with many tasks, much broader than their counterparts' work on airplanes. Not only did they maintain contact with the railway staff on board, but, serving as true tour guides, they would provide explanations of the landscape and places the train passed through, and they also acted as nannies and nurses. In short, they were "guardian angels" to each passenger. They thus became one of the train's biggest hallmarks and remained in service from 1949 to 1970, when the California Zephyr ceased to operate.

In 1983, Amtrak, the company created by the federal government to counter the decline of passenger rail transport, decided to revive the service, essentially following the original route of the "old" train. This time as well, even without the legendary Zephyrettes, the service has proven a great success, establishing itself as a journey to be taken at least once in a lifetime.

The California Zephyr travels a distance of 3,924 kilometers (2,438 miles) between Chicago and Emeryville, a town in the San Francisco metropolitan area. The journey is fifty-two hours and ten minutes long heading west, taking thirty minutes less heading east, with the service running daily. The rolling stock is not from the train's time of origin, but it is still captivating thanks to its **bilevel Superliner coaches** in exposed stainless steel, pulled by a pair of General Electric GEP42DC diesel locomotives. Its configuration includes a baggage car, three or four sleeping cars, a dining car, a lounge car with a panoramic dome, and two or three cars with reclining seats.

Passengers can elect to travel on normal seats which are wide and reclining. This is certainly the cheapest option but not exactly ideal for a fifty-two-hour journey. The preferred solution for those traveling the full distance is the two-seater cabin, called a "roomette," which transforms the two sofas into comfortable berths at night and also has meals included in its price. Of course, there are also real, larger bed compartments, ranging up to those for families (2 adults and 2 children up to twelve years old) and accessible cabins for people with wheelchairs.

The California Zephyr crosses seven states and makes thirty-five stops along its route from Illinois to California in a series of diverse landscapes.

The westward journey begins at Chicago Union Station in the early afternoon. While in Illinois (apart from Chicago, of course), the city of Galesburg, with a museum dedicated to the railroad, might be of interest to train enthusiasts. The Mississippi River marks the

transition between Illinois and Iowa. On its right bank lies the small town of Burlington. It is worth a visit, in part for the famous river, and for a strange curiosity: the town boasts the "most crooked" street in the world, with the (unsurprising) name of Snake Alley.

The characteristically peaceful Midwestern landscape, cornfields, cattle, and farms, pass by the train windows as it continues into Nebraska. There, the California Zephyr reaches Omaha. The city is also on a famous river, the Missouri, where, among other things, one can admire one of the few still extant "Big Boys" exhibited at the Lauritzen Gardens. These Union Pacific steam locomotives were the **largest and most powerful ever built** in the world.

Leaving Nebraska, the train enters Colorado, stopping for half an hour in the city of Denver to refuel the locomotives. Known as the "mile-high" city, Denver's official elevation is indeed exactly one mile (1.6km) above sea level. But the best is yet to come as the snow-

There is also another famous Zephyr in the history of U.S. railways. The Pioneer Zephyr, a diesel-powered train set made up of three articulated cars, was built by the Budd Company in 1934 for the Chicago, Burlington and Quincy Railroad (CB&Q). This set was the first diesel-powered streamliner to be built for mainline service in the United States. The cars were made of stainless steel and permanently connected via Jacobs bogies. It set a speed record for travel between Denver and Chicago on May 26, 1934, covering 1,633 kilometers (1,015 miles) in thirteen hours and five minutes without stopping, at an average speed of nearly 124 km/h (78 mph). The historic ride inspired a 1934 film called *The Silver Streak*, which would become the nickname of the train.

capped peaks of the Rocky Mountains rise behind the skyscrapers.

The locomotives push their engines to their maximum, and the train begins a long climb, amid a breathtaking landscape, up to the Moffat Tunnel, which is just over 10 kilometers (6 miles) long and about 2,825 kilometers (9,240 miles) above sea level at the route's highest point. Immediately after exiting the tunnel, the train stops at the municipality of Winter Park, from which the area's ski resorts can be accessed.

The train resumes its journey through the canyons of Colorado, just alongside the river, and its curves are so tight that passengers can see the front of the train from their windows. The pass inside Glenwood Canyon, about 20 kilometers (13 miles) long, is spectacular.

The California Zephyr enters Utah, and the landscape again changes, bringing a series of arid hills on the edge of a flat landscape that turns to desert upon arrival in Nevada. The train also stops in Winnemucca, a city that would be completely unknown had the local bank not been **robbed by Butch Cassidy** in 1900.

We finally arrive in California, but before descending to San Francisco and the Bay Area, the train still has the Sierra Nevada mountains to climb, crossing the Donner Pass. The Zephyr stops for only a few minutes in Sacramento, California's capital, but if you can, a visit to the California State Railroad Museum would hardly be a bad choice.

The train is now on level ground. Near Oakland, the train runs alongside the ocean before it enters the Emeryville terminal station. From here, passengers board Amtrak buses, which will take them to downtown San Francisco. The silhouette of the Golden Gate Bridge can already be seen in the distance.

34/35 – The California Zephyr takes on the large curve outside of Green River, Utah, pulled by two Amtrak diesel locomotives.

34 – The entrance to the Moffat Tunnel in Rollinsville, Colorado: this railroad tunnel crosses the Continental Divide and has been open to traffic since 1928.

35 – The Golden Gate Bridge, symbol of San Francisco, is suspended over the strait that connects the Pacific Ocean to San Francisco Bay.

Durango and Silverton Narrow Gauge Railroad

The epic of the West lives again in one of the most scenic steam train lines in the United States, running between Durango and Silverton, Colorado.

The **Durango and Silverton Narrow Gauge Railroad** (D&SNG) is a narrow, three-foot-gauge tourist and heritage line that operates along 72 kilometers (45 miles) of track between the towns of Durango and Silverton in Colorado. It is one of the most famous tourist railways in the world, for both the Old West aesthetic of its magnificent steam locomotives and coaches, and because it has starred or featured in dozens of movies and television shows. It has also been designated a National Historic Landmark by the United States federal government.

The railroad is unique, not only because of its spectacular route high in the mountains and its original rolling stock, but also because it has been in continuous service since 1882—it is likely the only U.S. line to have witnessed the regular use of steam locomotives from its inception up to the present day.

The route was opened in 1882 by the Denver and Rio Grande Western Railway (D&RG) to mostly transport silver, with some gold ore, mined from the San Juan Mountains. The line was an extension of D&RG's narrow gauge line, also a 914-mm (3-foot) gauge, from Antonito, Colorado, to Durango. A true rush to extract precious metal had boomed in the area, and the only way one could transport ore to the refineries and smelters in Durango, in an area without roads, was by train. The project was conceived by General William Palmer, who was an engineer, but more importantly was the head of the D&RG. Palmer was certain that the railroad to Silverton would be a great success, but he was aware of the technical challenges that its construction would entail. He therefore feared that the railroad's board of directors would not approve his project and thus decided to complete it in secret.

36 – Durango station, built in 1881. The railroad is now designated a National Historic Landmark.

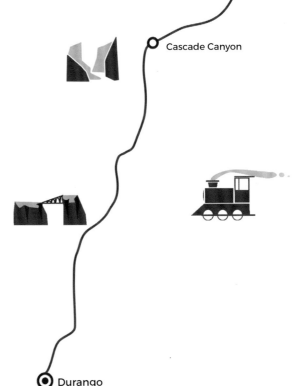

Silverton

Cascade Canyon

Durango

Departure: Durango
Arrival: Silverton
Distance: 72 km (45 miles)
Duration: 9 hours (round trip)
Stages: 1
Country: USA – Colorado

36/37 – This fantastic shot of a steam train on the Durango and Silverton Narrow Gauge Railroad, near Silverton, takes us back to the days of the Wild West.

PRACTICAL TIPS

THERE IS ALSO A TRAIN PULLED BY A DIESEL LOCOMOTIVE THAT
RUNS IN SUMMER. IT DEPARTS IN THE MORNING, TRANSPORTING
HIKERS TO STARTING POINTS FOR EXCURSIONS IN THE AREA,
THEN PICKING THEM UP IN THE AFTERNOON. APART FROM
REGULAR TOURIST TRAINS, SPECIAL TRAINS ARE OFTEN AVAILABLE
IN SUMMER AND WINTER FOR EVENTS AND DEMONSTRATIONS,
INCLUDING SPECIAL TRAINS FOR TAKING PHOTOS.

USEFUL WEBSITES
Durango and Silverton Narrow Gauge Railroad:
https://www.durangotrain.com

INTERESTING FACTS

The D&SNG Museum, opened in 1998, is a tribute to
American railroads and to southwestern Colorado. The
museum is situated in the Durango roundhouse. Half of
the roundhouse is used for steam locomotives running
on the line, while the other half houses the museum. The
museum houses numerous objects from D&RG and from
other railways, and it features many artifacts from the
Durango and Silverton areas. There is an HO-scale model
railway system in the museum representing a narrow-
gauge railroad similar to the D&RG. There is also a coach
used for movie filming, which featured in *Butch Cassidy and
the Sundance Kid*, with educational films about the railway
screened inside. Locomotive No. 478 is also held here,
awaiting its return to service. Part of the station in Silverton
has also been transformed into a museum displaying
objects from the period.

Such an initiative is simply unthinkable today, but in the American West of the late 1800s, it was possible. All information on its construction was kept confidential, and even photographs were forbidden while it was being built. Palmer, who was an excellent engineer, managed to find a way to take the train to Silverton by installing the track to climb along the steep sides of the valley traveled by the Animas River. Work was completed in July 1882, just eleven months after the railroad to Durango from Antonito was built. Early on, travel on the Durango–Silverton line was truly significant, with up to eight trains heading in both directions per day. Later, unfortunately, a federal measure put an end to the indiscriminate extraction of silver, causing its price to drop, beginning the line's slow decline. It should be noted, in any case, that during its very beginnings, the first seed of a tourist service was planted on the Durango and Silverton. More would be planted, and more significantly, by the 1950s. Since 1998, following several changes in ownership, the line has been in the hands of American Heritage Railways, which has given the line an enormous boost.

Its route contains no bridges, viaducts, or tunnels of particular importance, as such structures was avoided to speed up construction times and contain costs, but it is absolutely spectacular. This is because the tracks, to be able to ascend from an altitude of 1,984 meters (6,512 feet) in Durango to 2,836 meters (9,318 feet) in Silverton, were laid along sheer cliffs above the river in a position that was extremely difficult to execute. The train makes its way laboriously, never exceeding 30 km/h (18 mph), toward Silverton, yard by yard.

There are nine steam locomotives available, eight of them in service, with many cars from the same period. The line is in operation throughout the year, but the number of trains in circulation, naturally, increases in summertime. In the summer, from May to October, the train travels the full 72 kilometers (45 miles) to Silverton, while in winter, train excursions end at Cascade station, 41 kilometers (26 miles) from Durango. The steam train runs daily, departing in the morning and arriving in Silverton soon after midday.

During the stop, which is about two hours long, passengers can watch the impressive process of turning the locomotive around on a depot turntable. The train then departs in mid-afternoon and arrives in Durango in the early evening. There are three levels of service, and passengers have the choice of traveling in one of the heritage cars or one of the newer **open-air gondola coaches**, which, thanks in part to the low speed, allow travelers to immerse themselves in their surroundings and enjoy the beautiful landscape to its fullest.

38 – A steam train travels the Durango and Silverton Narrow Gauge Railroad, skirting the Animas Canyon in the San Juan National Forest.

39 top – A train travels along the Durango and Silverton Narrow Gauge Railroad, surrounded by autumn colors.

39 center – The scenic railroad track to Silverton through Colorado's San Juan Mountains.

39 bottom – Apart from the cars, the railroad terminus in Silverton is still very similar to the station of the 1800s.

Great Smoky Mountains Railroad

Excursions in North Carolina, aboard one of the United States' most popular heritage railways.

The **Great Smoky Mountains Railroad** (GSMR), is a heritage railroad based chiefly in Bryson City, North Carolina. It is owned and operated by American Heritage Railways Inc., which also operates another famous heritage railroad, the Durango and Silverton Narrow Gauge Railroad.

Owing to its route and the landscape it navigates, the GSMR is one of the most popular heritage tourist railways in the United States. This line follows the route of the major Southern Railway company's former Murphy branch line, whose construction dates back to 1891. It features numerous bridges and sections with grades of up to 5%, something truly remarkable for **a railway relying on natural adhesion**. Much of the line runs along the banks of the Little Tennessee and Nantahala Rivers, and one of the most spectacular moments is while crossing Fontana Lake, accomplished via a bridge with four spans, about 238 meters (780 feet) long and 30 meters (100 feet) high. The line traveled by GSMR trains is 85 kilometers (53 miles) long, passing through Dillsboro, Bryson City, and Nantahala. The original track once continued onward to Murphy but is no longer in service. Although mainly a tourist line, the GSMR continues to transport freight for some factories in the area thanks to an interchange with the Blue Ridge Southern Railroad in Sylva. It also runs beyond the tourist destination of Nantahala, to Andrews.

The tourist service uses a magnificent **S160 steam locomotive**, no.1702, originally built for the U.S. Army in 1942, and four diesel locomotives from the same era: a GP7 no.711, GP9 nos.1751 and 1755, and a GP30 no.2467. The service runs throughout the year, also offering various excursions that can be combined with the rail route.

Departure: Dillsboro
Arrival: Nantahala
Distance: 85 km (53 miles)
Duration: From 2 hours and 30 to 5 hours
Stages: 1 (with several excursions)
Country: USA – North Carolina

40 – The GSMR S160-class locomotive no. 1702, built in 1942 for the U.S. Army, is one of this heritage railroad's main attractions.

41 – The four-span bridge, 230 meters (425 feet) long, that extends across Fontana Lake is one of the most spectacular points along the line.

PRACTICAL TIPS

ALL THE VARIOUS EXCURSION TRAINS DEPART FROM
THE BRYSON CITY STATION.
THE RAILWAY IS ACTIVE THROUGHOUT THE YEAR,
WITH MORE TRAINS RUNNING IN SUMMER. CONSULT
THE ONLINE CALENDAR OF DEPARTURES, WHICH IS
KEPT UP TO DATE.

USEFUL WEBSITES
Great Smoky Mountains Railroad:
https://www.gsmr.com

42 – S160-class locomotive no. 1702 heads a tourist train along the Tuckasegee River on an excursion to view the fall colors in the valley's woods.

43 left – Whitewater rafting on the Nantahala River, as seen from the train.

43 right – A view from the train of Fontana Lake and the Great Smoky Mountains near Bryson City.

Without question, the local mountains are the main attraction in winter, while in spring, special the railroad offers extra activities that continue through summer. One could, for example, **combine a train ticket with a rafting trip** or a breathtaking zipline flight. In autumn, some special trains take passengers to admire the magnificent foliage in the woods heading toward the Nantahala Gorge.

The railroad offers a variety of round-trip scenic excursions departing from Bryson City. These trips vary from two and a half to five hours of adventure.

The Nantahala Gorge Excursion, for example, takes passengers 70 kilometers (44 miles) to the Gorge, where hikers can explore the Little Tennessee River and Fontana Lake before returning. The excursion on the Tuckasegee River, on the other hand, travels a

INTERESTING FACTS

The S160-class steam locomotive no. 1702, which GSMR purchased and returned to service, boasts an interesting record, being the only locomotive of this group still functioning in the United States. This is all the more surprising considering that it forms part of the largest group of steam locomotives ever built in the United States, numbering a good 2,120 models. It was built by Baldwin Locomotive Works for the U.S. Army during World War II, in September 1942. After several changes of ownership, it was purchased by GSMR in 1991. It ran until 2005, when it was decommissioned due to firebox issues. In 2012, the GSMR entered into an agreement with Swain County (NC), taking a $700,000 loan for the construction of a new steam locomotive workshop and restoration of the no. 1702, which returned to service in July 2016.

52-kilometer (32-mile) route, stopping at old railway towns scattered among the wide, grassy slopes. In Bryson City you can also visit the **Smoky Mountain Trains Museum,** which displays a wonderful collection of antique Lionel railway models as well as a large-scale moving train model. It also houses a large train model shop, with themed souvenirs and books.

GSMR trains offer various levels of service. The highest is First Class, sold only to travelers over twenty-one, providing a lounge car with assigned dining table seats, air-conditioning, souvenirs, and free drinks. The Premium Open Air Gondola is also only available for passengers over twenty-one and is essentially an open-air car (with a protective roof in case of rain), with two rows of seats in the center, facing outward back-to-back. Crown and Coach Classes are

in regular cars with two seats on either side of the central aisle, large windows, and air-conditioning. They are available to all ages. The only differences between the two are that Crown Class has assigned seats and passengers receive a souvenir tumbler and free drinks. Finally, there is an Open Air Gondola whose seats are more spartan than the first class counterpart, with access open to all.

On the return trip passengers are invited to move to the opposite side of their car to get a different perspective on the scenery.

Tickets for all train classes pulled by the steam locomotive include a surcharge for the higher running and maintenance costs compared to a diesel locomotive. For travelers who do not receive a served lunch, boxed lunches are available and can be booked in advance.

El Chepe Express and Regional

El Chepe Express, from Los Mochis to Chihuahua through Mexico's Copper Canyon and Las Cascadas National Park.

Departure: Los Mochis
Arrival: Chihuahua
Distance: 673 km (418 miles)
Duration: 16 hours on the full regional route, 9 hours on the tourist train
Stages: 3 (tourist train)
Country: Mexico

El Chepe Express is a tourist train that, within a nine-hour journey, travels over 350 kilometers (215 miles) into the heart of the Sierra Tarahumara, across the natural wonder of the Copper Canyon and the other deep canyons lying between the states of Sinaloa and Chihuahua in northern Mexico. The El Chepe Express route departs from Los Mochis and arrives in Creel, stopping in the cities of El Fuerte, Bahuichivo, and Divisadero. In some places, the train is the only possible means of crossing and visiting the area. El Chepe Express travels along the southwestern tracks of the Ferrocarril Chihuahua al Pacífico (Chihuahua-Pacific Railway), a 673-kilometer (418-mile) railroad line that connects the city of Chihuahua to Los Mochis and the nearby port of Topolobampo on the Pacific.

The line carries significant freight traffic, with the **El Chepe Regional** train also running in addition to the El Chepe Express tourist train, serving the area's inhabitants. It is one of only three passenger rail services that remain active in Mexico, apart from commuter services in Mexico City. The other two are the Tequila Express, which connects Guadalajara to the city of Tequila (the birthplace of Mexico's most well-known drink) in the state of Jalisco, and the Tijuana-Tecate service in Baja California.

The line winds dramatically, its route rising from sea level to nearly 2,400 meters (8,000 feet) above near Divisadero, a place owing its name to its location on the Continental Divide and an excellent lookout spot to view the Copper Canyon. To complete the trip, thirty-seven bridges and eighty-six tunnels, including spiral tunnels, were built to quickly gain altitude. It takes sixteen hours to cover El Chepe Regional's entire route.

The construction of this railway line, conceived as early as 1880, began at the beginning of the twentieth century. Due both to financial issues and to difficulties encountered on the

44 – The spectacular Basaseachic Falls, in the national park of the same name, is the second highest waterfall in Mexico, 246 meters (807 feet) high.

45 – One of the mighty Ferromex diesel locomotives at the head of the tourist train "El Chepe Express," not far from the Copper Canyon.

PRACTICAL TIPS

TO RESERVE A SEAT ON EL CHEPE REGIONAL
(TOURIST CLASS ONLY), PHONE THE CALL CENTER
AT (800) 122-4373 OR MAKE A DIRECT CALL TO
THE STATION TICKET OFFICE.

USEFUL WEBSITES
The only official website of Chepe Express:
https://chepe.mx

46 – An impressive view of the Copper Canyon, the group of six distinct canyons in the Sierra Madre Occidental, carved by six rivers flowing from the mountain range.

extremely rough terrain, however, construction was not completed until 1961.

In 1998, the private railroad company Ferromex took over management of both passenger and freight services. The frequency of trains and train times may vary, so it is useful to check for information before planning a trip. El Chepe Express, the train reserved exclusively for tourists, currently travels three times per week between Creel and Los Mochis, offering passengers two levels of service, the more affordable Tourist Class and the Executive, which is more exclusive and expensive.

El Chepe Regional, on the other hand, covers all 673 kilometers (418 miles) of the route between Chihuahua, Creel, and Los Mochis three times a week, with three levels of service: Tourist, Regional, and Economy Class. However, El Chepe Regional's tourist admission rules may change: El Chepe Regional only just began to allow tourists on board again as of May 1, 2021, with some restrictions. Effectively, one can travel on El Chepe Regional if a section of El Chepe Express has been booked, provided that the leg booked on El Chepe Express is longer than that section on El Chepe Regional.

El Chepe Express is designed to be a **luxury tourist service**, while El Chepe Regional allows travelers to immerse themselves further in local life and customs. The choice depends not only on the budget available but also on the type of trip and experience preferred.

On El Chepe Express, travelers will find a club car with a panoramic terrace and a bar car with panoramic windows. There is a luxury dining car with a restaurant, reserved for Executive and First Classes, its menu inspired by local cuisine and carefully curated by famous Mexican chefs Danile Ovadia and Salvator Orozco. There is a second dining car for Tourist Class passengers.

In addition to their panoramic windows, Executive Class cars offer reclining seats, a bar, high-resolution screens, and a high-quality audio system, while the First Class ticket price also includes an onboard lunch with preferred access to the restaurant and the panoramic terrace bar. Tourist Class offers comfortable armchairs and a service of snacks and drinks on board. In any case, the El Chepe Express ticket allows travelers to alight at three stations of their choice along the route. If the total journey takes about nine hours, passengers can then decide whether and how to break the journey up into several stages, having the option to stop at an intermediate station to explore the area. At each location, one can select accommodation for a stay of several nights.

The landscape traversed by the train is among the most beautiful imaginable. **The Copper Canyon area alone is worth the trip**: the

47 left – A photo of the valley traversed by the Ferrocarril Chihuahua al Pacífico, making a wide 180-degree bend near Témoris.

47 top right – The Church of San Francisco Javier in Cerocahui, a village in the Sierra Tarahumara near the Copper Canyon.

47 bottom right – The spectacular suspended walkway in Divisadero offering a panoramic view of the Copper Canyon.

canyon complex is four times as long as the United States' Grand Canyon and in some places is twice as deep. But what is unique is the entire network of canyons crossed, from the driest areas to other, greener spots, together with the winding, daring path of the train.

No less interesting are the cities where El Chepe Express stops. Los Mochis is the third largest city by population in the state of Sinaloa, and its name is thought to refer to a local species of turtle. It offers, among other things, a visit to the Church of the Sacred Heart of Jesus and the beautiful Botanical Garden. It is only about 30 kilometers (18 miles) from the sea, and in the Topolobampo Bay, visitors can take part in underwater fishing and other sporting activities.

After traveling for a further hour and a half, El Chepe stops in El Fuerte, which takes its name from a fort built by the Spanish in 1610. Here, must-visit attractions include the House of General Pablo Macias, the cathedral, the central plaza, and the House of Culture. The prehistoric rock carvings in nearby Cerro de la Mascara are highly interesting.

Then comes Bahuichivo station, from which the small town of Cerocahui, founded in 1860 by Jesuit missionaries, can be reached. The area is tranquil and green, offering a magnificent overview from the summit of Cerro del Gallego at an altitude of about 1,879 meters (6,165 feet). From there, you can admire the depth of the barranca, the town of Urique, and the river that meanders behind.

Divisadero is a must for travelers on El Chepe Express (and those who have chosen El Chepe Regional). From there, one can take in a **panoramic view of three canyons**: the Copper Canyon, the Tararecua Canyon, and the Urique Canyon. Visitors can walk along the top of the canyons to appreciate their natural beauty even more closely.

Finally, Creel is the final destination of El Chepe Express (while the Regional continues up to Chihuahua), and its point of departure in the opposite direction. From there, one can visit Mexico's most impressive waterfalls in Las Cascadas National Park. The Piedra Volada Falls are among these, with a height of 456 meters (1,485 feet)—and they are magnificent, especially in the rainy season. Several valleys around the city are also named for the curious local rock formations, including the "Valley of the Frogs," the "Valley of the Nuns," and the "Valley of Mushrooms."

El Chepe, both the Express and Regional, run throughout the year, so the region can always be visited. The winter period between December and March is best for those who would like to combine the train ride with hiking experiences, especially in the canyons, which in summer can reach temperatures of around 50 degrees Celsius (120 degrees Fahrenheit) at the bottom. It must also be kept in mind that these are still the high mountains. In Creel, elevated about 2,300 meters (7,500 feet) above sea level, it often snows in winter. Summertime, in contrast, between June and August, is the rainiest season in this region, which poses a problem for visitors planning to hike. The landscape, on the other hand, is much more lush. Spring and autumn are the best times—but only so long as one has the foresight to avoid the time of Holy Week in spring, which is always very crowded.

48 – One of thirty-seven scenic bridges testifying to the challenge and complexity of El Chepe's route.

48/49 – The Valle de Ongos ("Valley of Mushrooms") is one of the Sierra Madre Occidental's most impressive attractions. The varying density of the rock, when eroded, has given life to curious formations.

PERU

CUSCO TO
AGUA CALIENTES
AND PUNO

Departure: Cusco
Arrival: Agua Calientes
Distance: 113 km (70 miles)
Duration: From 3 hours 15 minutes
to 4 hours and 40 minutes
Stages: 1
Country: Peru

Departure: Cusco
Arrival: Puno
Distance: 385 km (239 miles)
Duration: 10 hours
Stages: 1
Country: Peru

50/51 – A view of the lost Inca city of Machu Picchu, near Cusco: Machu Picchu is a Peruvian Historic Sanctuary and a UNESCO World Heritage Site.

PeruRail and Inca Rail

Nearly touching the sky in the land of the Incas: to Machu Picchu and Lake Titicaca.

The archaeological site of **Machu Picchu** and **Lake Titicaca** are two of Peru's top tourist destinations. This is especially true of the first. Often interpreted to mean "old mountain" in the Quechua language, the site is universally known for its imposing Inca ruins: it is listed as a UNESCO World Heritage Site and in 2007 was voted one of the new seven wonders of the world. It thus comes as no surprise that, while it is not as easily accessible as other famous places in the world, the site is visited by hundreds of thousands of tourists every year, the impact of which is concerning, and not only for its preservation.

In the attempt to manage and organize this continuous flow of people, who provide a fundamental contribution to the economy of Peru and to the region, **the railway is the principal means of access** to Machu Picchu.

A train ride, to visit first the archaeological site and then Lake Titicaca farther south, is a fascinating experience, in part for the splendor of the territories traversed, as well as their history.

The railroad lines in this region form what was called the Ferrocarriles del Sur (Peru Southern Railway) and were built at different times. In 1876, the rail line was opened to traffic from the city of Matarani on the coast, passing through Arequipa and Juliaca to Puno, where ferries would depart for Bolivia across Lake Titicaca. In 1908, the line heading north from Juliaca to Cusco was completed. The 113-kilometer (70-mile) leg between

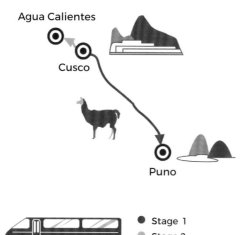

Agua Calientes

Cusco

Puno

● Stage 1
● Stage 2

51 – A woman in traditional dress, walking along the shores of Lake Titicaca.

Cusco and Agua Calientes, the terminal station and access point to Machu Picchu, was built gradually in sections and inaugurated in 1928. One matter of note is that, while all the other lines are standard-gauge, at 1,435 millimeters (4 feet, 8½ inches), only the Cusco – Agua Calientes was built with, and still has, a narrow gauge of 914 millimeters (3 feet). This was to facilitate its construction in the area's rugged mountains, and the line is therefore separated from the others.

Today, the tracks belong to the Peruvian state, and the service is

entrusted to two competing railway companies, **PeruRail** and **Inca Rail**. Both offer tourist trains from Cusco to Agua Calientes, to visit Machu Picchu, and to other different destinations, including Lake Titicaca. Naturally, the quality of the trips offered varies broadly, ranging from a good tourist class to high luxury.

PeruRail also has a "local" train that runs between Cusco and Agua Calientes, which is of course very affordable and "authentic," since it is used by local residents. Unfortunately, non-Peruvians are not allowed to travel on this train. The official reason is to reserve the train for those who live and work there, but it is likely not too far-fetched to infer an economic reason given the cost of tourist tickets, even the less luxurious ones. The matter is complex: one certainly travels comfortably on a tourist train, yet isolated in a "bubble" of sorts, seeing only the Peru of brochures and the expected folklore.

PeruRail and Inca Rail are both private companies. While it will not be possible here to describe each of the various services offered in detail, the various routes can be mentioned, as it is not actually necessary to depart from Cusco in order to arrive in Agua Calientes.

The longer historic route departs from the Cusco San Pedro station. The station is in the city center, but trains currently only use

52 top left – The sun rises over the Plaza de Armas, Cusco's main square and the heart of the city.

52 center left – A train of the Inca Rail company coming from Cusco to Agua Calientes station.

52 bottom left – A rainy day for tourists heading to Agua Calientes, the town where the archaeological site of Machu Picchu can be accessed.

the station between 5 and 7 a.m., since **trains passing through the city have become a safety hazard**. For this reason, most trains depart from the Cusco Poroy station about 15 kilometers (9 miles) from the city. Those trains, however, no longer travel one of the truly characteristic points of the line, the zigzag that the railway makes before reaching Poroy. At this stage of the route, the train moves back and forth for half an hour, running on stretches of track in opposing directions at a strong incline. This allows the train to gain altitude quickly without having to extend the line or to make 180-degree turns, as there is absolutely no space for such turns on the mountainside.

Buses are available to take passengers from the center of Cusco to the Poroy station when the train is not able to use the central station. One can alternatively depart from the city of Urubamba, which lies on a short secondary branch of the main line, or from the Ollantaytambo station, both locations close to the final station of Agua Calientes.

When choosing between PeruRail and Inca Rail, it is useful to visit the companies' websites, which are full of images and explanations. Overall, PeruRail has more experience behind it, since it began its

52 right – The luxurious interior of the PeruRail train heading from Cusco to Puno on Lake Titicaca.

53 – A PeruRail train in the station at Agua Calientes, from where travelers can reach Machu Picchu.

 PRACTICAL TIPS

USEFUL WEBSITES
Operators:
PeruRail (Cusco – Machu Picchu, Cusco – Puno/Lake Titicaca)
https://www.perurail.com

Inca Rail (Cusco – Machu Picchu trains only)
https://www.incarail.com

Tourist information:
https://www.peru.info

Access to the archaeological area of Machu Picchu is limited, so you must first secure your tickets there, and only then purchase train tickets. Tickets can be purchased in advance on the website www.machupicchu.gob.pe or in Cusco at the National Cultural Institute (INC) at Avenida La Cultura 238. Since 2011, the number of visitors has been limited to 2,500 per day, about the number expected on a typical day in a busy month like June, but less than the number of visitors that used to come in peak months. Entrance tickets are timed, from 06:30 to 12:00 or from 12:00 to 17:30, so be sure of your admission time before booking train tickets. If you book in advance on the website, you will be able to print your ticket.

operations in 1999, while Inca Rail was founded in in 2007.

PeruRail offers tourist services not only to Machu Picchu but also to Puno for a visit to Lake Titicaca. Heading to Machu Picchu, three types of service are available: they are, in ascending order of the service level on each train, the Expedition, the Vistadome, and the Hiram Bingham (luxury) train. Traveling from Cusco to Puno are the Titicaca and the Andean Explorer, the latter being the first luxury sleeper train in South America.

Setting aside these luxury trains, whose level of service is akin to that of similar European lines, PeruRail offers coaches with large windows on both sides and on the ceiling, as well as a panoramic coach with an open terrace for admiring the astonishing Andean landscape. Let us remember that these areas have elevations between 3,400 meters (11,152 feet) above sea level in Cusco and 3,800 meters (12,500 feet) in Puno on Lake Titicaca, and that nearby Mount Ausangate reaches 6,384 meters (20,945 feet).

Inca Rail, operating only on the line from Cusco to Machu Picchu, offers four different rail services: they are, in ascending order of quality and cost, the Voyager, the 360°, the First Class, and the Private, an exclusive luxury train. Facilities and services are similar to its competition's

54/55 A magnificent image taken from the PeruRail train connecting the city of Cusco with the town of Puno on Lake Titicaca.

54 – In the "observatory" coach at the end of the PeruRail train from Cusco to Puno, passengers can admire the vast Andean Plateau.

55 – Traditional reed boats on Lake Titicaca near Puno.

and, like PeruRail's are of good quality.

To travel to this part of South America without visiting the shores of Lake Titicaca, which alongside Machu Picchu is considered a place connected to the Inca civilization's origins, would be a true shame. The journey from Cusco to Puno with PeruRail's Titicaca train is 385 kilometers (240 miles) long and lasts about ten hours, crossing Peru's Central Andean Plateau. Trees cannot grow at such heights, so the landscape is marked by a kind of steppe, dotted with small villages and farms. The train stops in the town of La Raya, whose station, at 4,319 meters (over 14,000 feet), is the **highest in the world used for a regular passenger service**. The train travels three times a week in each direction, with a departure early in the morning and arriving at its destination in the afternoon. This allows visitors to savor the heart of these ancient lands in a more genuine, less tourist-centered atmosphere than the beautiful area around Machu Pichu.

ARGENTINA

ESQUEL TO NAHUEL PAN
EL MAITÉN TO INGENIERO
BRUNO THOMAE

Departure: Esquel
Arrival: Nahuel Pan
Distance: 20 km (12.5 miles)
Duration: 2 hours 30 minutes
Stages: 1
Country: Argentina

Departure: El Maitén
Arrival: Ingeniero Bruno Thomae
Distance: 27 km (18 miles)
Duration: 2 hours 30 minutes
Stages: 1
Country: Argentina

56/57 – One of the century-old steam locomotives still in service on the line at Nahuel Pan station.

La Trochita

In Patagonia, Argentina, the steam train that fascinated Luis Sepúlveda still travels between Esquel and El Maitén.

Patagonia, Argentina, is truly at the edge of the world, geographically and in the public imagination. Only Antarctica lies farther south. Traveling through Patagonia on **La Trochita**, a steam train from a century past that has remained the same to the present day, is an unforgettable experience.

The novelist Paul Theroux was so impressed by the route that he named his book about his train journeys in the Americas *The Old Patagonian Express*. This train also fascinated the writer Luis Sepúlveda, who says in his book *Patagonia Express*: "'Here it is, gentlemen, the old Patagonia Express. Do you want to take a ride?' one of the rail workers asked. … 'The gringos have gone north, so we will go south,' said the driver."

La Trochita, whose official name is the Viejo Expreso Patagónico (**Old Patagonian Express**) resists the sirens of globalized tourism and offers an opportunity to go beyond the view of the landscape. It allows passengers to rediscover the Patagonia of another time, a place that in the past two centuries was the destination of rugged men and courageous women, chasing the last frontier on the edge of the world, in an environment as beautiful as it is hostile. Today, the train brings in hardened travelers, train enthusiasts, and tourists, all in search of an extraordinary experience.

The nickname "La Trochita" comes from the term trocha angosta, or "narrow path," referring to the narrow gauge of the track selected for constructing the line, just 750 millimeters (30 inches). La Trochita's original route stretched 402 kilometers (250 miles) from the Esquel station to that of Ingeniero Jacobacci, 242 kilometers (150 miles) to the northeast of El Maitén.

This northern terminus of the line is named in honor of Guido Jacobacci, the Italian engineer (originally from Modena) who designed and managed the Patagonian railway network on behalf of the Argentine government

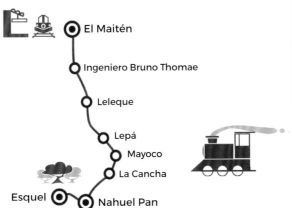

57 – The Spartan interior of La Trochita's only first-class coach. The coal stove that heats it in winter is clearly visible on the left.

in 1908. In January 1925, inhabitants of the remote area, at about the 278th mile of the San Antonio Oeste – Nahuel Huapi line, chose to name their colony and station "Engineer Jacobacci" in memory of this railwayman who had taken them, at least in part, out of isolation.

In addition to the two termini, fourteen other stations were built along the tracks, with the primary one, almost in the middle of the route, being El Maitén. Up until regular operations ended in 1992, following a progressive decline beginning in the mid-1960s, a **"flagstop" service** was in place along the line—in other words, those who wished to get on the train at any point would simply wave a piece of light-colored cloth, and the driver would stop the train, which was **only traveling at 45 km/h (28 mph)**.

The end of this service sparked fierce protest, not only in Patagonia, but throughout Argentina and the rest of the world, where in the meantime La Trochita had become famous. The Argentine government backtracked, and in 1998, it declared the line, its locomotives, and its cars a National Historic Monument.

Today, there are **three options** for traveling along the La Trochita line, all aimed at tourists. The most frequent excursion is from Esquel to the village of Nahuel Pan, which takes about an hour each way. The train travels some 20 kilometers (12.5 miles) along the slopes of the hills surrounding the city, then passes through the valley at the foot of Nahuel Pan Hill. After crossing National Route 40, it enters the territory of the Mapuche-Tehuelche Nahuel Pan community. At the village, there is a forty-five minutes stop. The train maneuvers in preparation for its return journey, while passengers can visit the Museum of Native Patagonian Culture, craft fairs, and the Tokom Topayiñ Fair, which all open upon the train's arrival. Depending on the season, this train runs from two to three times up to six times per week.

A second excursion, with guides on board the train, departs from El Maitén station to Ingeniero Bruno Thomae and back, with the trip lasting about two and a half hours. Both Esquel and El Maitén also offer exhibits on the history of the train, which can be viewed before or after the trip.

Finally, an exciting option for groups of train enthusiasts is the possibility of **chartering La Trochita** for a private journey, either from Esquel to El Maitén, or even further, from Esquel along the entire original route to Ingeniero Jacobacci. Renting the train needs to be booked at least six months in advance so that the railroad can check the tracks and make any necessary repairs.

La Trochita's rolling stock is of a bygone era, lovingly kept in operation by the railway workers, who proudly stress that "everything is original, as it once was." There are seven steam locomotives that are still in working order, but two are currently in service, both from 1922: a Henschel built in Germany, and a Baldwin built in the U.S. Both are **"Mikado" locomotives**, a term indicating the steam locomotives'

wheel arrangement. They have a front supporting axle, four coupled driving axles, and a rear supporting axle. The firebox is fueled using naphtha instead of coal, partially alleviating drivers' fatigue.

Even the coaches are original, with their wooden construction and small windows offering protection from the harsh local winter. There are simple wooden seats in each coach, and at the center of the car sits an old cast-iron stove, which the passengers themselves fuel with wood, providing heat in winter. A kettle full of hot water is always available on the stove, so travelers can prepare the characteristic Argentine yerba mate, a drink infused with the herb of the same name. The train has two more cars in its configuration, a "restaurant" and a first-class coach, which are also original but were built some years later, in 1955.

It goes without saying that a journey aboard such a train, peering at the landscape that is beautiful in both summer and winter, and witnessing the water and lubrication being applied to each of the locomotive's connecting rods at each stop, conjures the daily life of the railway a century ago.

INTERESTING FACTS

The city of Esquel is also the gateway to Los Alerces National Park, just about 40 kilometers (25 miles) away, considered one of the most beautiful in all of Argentina for its rich wooded and lake-filled landscape. Above all, the park protects and safeguards woods with Patagonian Cypress, a conifer locally called *alerce* or *lahuàn* in indigenous language. The tree is one of the longest-surviving on the planet and is at risk of extinction. Majestic specimens live along the shores of Lake Menéndez that are estimated to be about 4,000 years old, nearly 75 meters (250 feet) tall, with a diameter of 3.5 meters (11.5 feet). Indigenous cultures considered the tree to be sacred. Today, the park is one of the few areas where these incredible trees still live, and for this reason, it has been designated a UNESCO World Heritage Site since 2017.

58/59 – The enthralling landscape of the Argentine highlands being crossed by the Viejo Expreso Patagónico, which is exactly as it was a century ago.

Interrail Pass

The ticket for traveling freely through Europe: created fifty years ago for youth travelers and now available to all residents for use in thirty-three countries, to over 40,000 destinations.

Interrail may have turned fifty years old recently, but it has never been in such good shape. This combined ticket, which allows travelers to visit 40,000 destinations on railways (and ferries) in thirty-three European countries, is living a second youth. Born in 1972 as a concession for young people under twenty-one aiming to broaden their horizons and gain exposure to all European countries, today the pass is also a highly appreciated tool for adults and seniors (over sixty years old).

This is, certainly, in part due to its relative convenience over

purchasing individual tickets from each railroad operator in the countries visited. It is also due to an ever-increasing awareness of the train as a **greener means of transport** and one that, much more than an airplane, can reveal the cities and different parts of Europe as they really are. It is no coincidence that the ticket's popularity has even grown in the era of low-cost flights.

There are various types of Interrail pass, either first or second class, but they all have two things in common: the first is the ability to travel without route limits within a period of twenty-four hours for a set number of days, and the second is that pass holders need not decide on a fixed itinerary first, as one would need to if purchasing individual tickets. Instead, travelers can choose where to go and how many routes to cover from day to day. Tickets thus range from a pass for

travel without route limitations for a minimum of four chosen days in a given month up to a maximum of fifteen days. This tickets come in two formats: the **One Country Pass**, which, as the name implies, is used within just one country, or **Global Pass**, which includes all thirty-three countries taking part in the initiative. But that is not all: at a higher cost, of course, there are also Continuous Passes, tickets from fifteen days to three months, with which holders can take unlimited trips each day for the length of its validity—an Interrail pass for true globetrotters. There is also an ad hoc pass for ferries between the Greek islands.

All European or non-European nationals who legally reside in a European country can purchase an Interrail pass, and today, the age limits of the past are gone. There are currently four age groups that correspond to different prices for each type of pass: children between four and eleven years of age (who travel for free), young people ages twelve to twenty-seven, adults twenty-eight and older, and seniors, adults over sixty. Children younger than four travel for free (accompanied, of course) with no need for an Interrail pass.

All passes are available in paper or digital format and can be purchased either on the official website or via the traditional sales channels of railway companies, station ticket offices, and travel agencies. Whether the pass is digital, on one's smartphone, or on paper, each time travelers decide to make a trip, they must "upload" the route to be traveled, the date, and the departure and arrival times of the chosen train so crew members can confirm.

The digital pass also comes with a very useful app called Rail Planner, which allows travelers to consult the train timetables of all thirty-three countries, understand which of them need a reservation (and must be paid for separately), and plan itineraries. The Interrail pass allows holders to travel on every train, from local and regional lines to high-speed trains and night trains, but some of them require a seat reservation, which can be done through the same app. The app also highlights places where discounts are available to Interrail

Departure and Arrival: One of 40,000 European stations
Distance: 24,360 km (151,217 miles)
Duration: From 4 days to 3 months
Country: 33 European countries

pass holders, from hostels and local transport to museum entry.

Railroads of the following countries have joined Interrail: Austria, Belgium, Bosnia Herzegovina, Bulgaria, Croatia, the Czech Republic, Denmark, Estonia, Finland, France, Germany, Greece, Hungary, Ireland, Italy, Latvia, Lithuania, Luxembourg, Montenegro, the Netherlands, North Macedonia, Norway, Poland, Portugal, Romania, Serbia, Slovakia, Slovenia, Spain, Sweden, Switzerland, Turkey, and the United Kingdom. A traveler could start, for example, in Gällivare in Sweden's north, well beyond the Arctic Circle, having seen the midnight sun, then arrive in Palermo or Athens to enjoy the much warmer Mediterranean sun using the same ticket, deciding your itinerary and stops day by day.

INTERESTING FACTS

The Interrail Pass is one of the best concepts to ever be realized in Europe. The ticket is synonymous with singular experiences, and incomparably so, as it connects people, allows friendships to grow from encounters along the way, and offers much more than simple travel or a flight to a destination. Since the ticket was introduced in March 1972, more than 10 million people have used it to travel by train across the continent. Interrailers mainly travel from June to September. Travel destinations in southern and western Europe are popular, as are those in central Europe. The most frequent users are still young people, at 64%. In 2019, the last year prior to the Covid-19 pandemic, there was an increase of 20% in the number of pass buyers, which was in line with the trends of prior years, showing a growth of 78% among senior passengers.

The Orient Express

Departure: Paris
Arrival: Venice
Distance: 850 km (528 miles)
Duration: 2 days
Stages: 1
Country: France, Italy

The king of all trains returns to its Paris-Venice itinerary, transporting travelers back to the magical atmosphere of the Roaring '20s.

The **Orient Express** is without a doubt the most well-known and celebrated train in the world. It garnered its fame in the early decades of the twentieth century, when large luxury trains connecting European capitals were veritable five-star hotels on rails. The Orient Express was certainly the most beautiful and fascinating of all, in part for its route from the Gare de l'Est in Paris to Sirkeci station on Istanbul's European side, at the mouth of the Golden Horn.

Today, thanks to Belmond Management Ltd., a British company specializing in luxury tourism, the Orient Express has resumed its travels on European rails, with the same luxury coaches from a century ago, allowing passengers to travel back in time and relive the unique and legendary atmosphere that still fascinates every traveler. The itineraries offered each year, from March to November, are numerous, stopping at various European cities, but one of the classic routes is from London to Venice, or vice versa, the route once followed by the Venice Simplon Orient Express.

Before diving into the enchanted world of this exclusive tourist train, the history of the Orient Express must briefly be retraced. It began on October 4, 1883, when the CIWL (Compagnie Internationale des Wagons-Lits), conceived and founded by the Belgian engineer Georges Nagelmackers, inaugurated a **luxury train** between Paris and Constantinople (now Istanbul). The route was a success from the very start, both for the exotic charm of its destination city and for the quality of the service offered, which was unthinkable from other trains of the time. The journey soon became an experience that could not be missed by aristocrats, ambassadors, descendants of the upper middle class, and businessmen. The outbreak of the First World War forced the train to cease operations for the first time, but it resumed its travels in 1919, once the conflict was over.

62 top – An iconic brass logo with two rampant lions, which has been the trademark of the Compagnie Internationale des Wagons-Lits since its founding.

62 bottom – Two ex-CIWL coaches with their historic blue livery and white roof, now part of the Orient Express lineup and ready to welcome passengers aboard.

63 – One of six elegant posters designed by Pierre Fix-Masseau for the 1983 Orient Express advertising campaign.

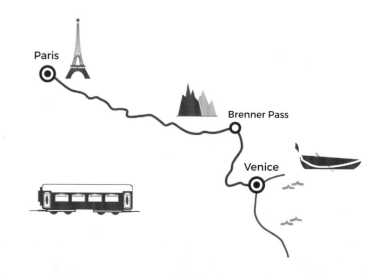

Paris

Brenner Pass

Venice

FIX-MASSEAU 85

COLLECTION
VENICE SIMPLON
ORIENT-EXPRESS
PARIS

THE VENICE SIMPLON ORIENT EXPRESS TRAVELS ACROSS EUROPE WITH VARIOUS DESTINATIONS AND ITINERARIES FROM MARCH TO NOVEMBER. THE TRIP TO ISTANBUL IS MADE JUST ONCE A YEAR.

USEFUL WEBSITES
Venice Simplon Orient Express:
**https://www.belmond.com/it/trains/europe
/venice-simplon-orient-express**

The twenty years that followed, leading up to the beginning of the Second World War in 1939, were the most wonderful aboard the Orient Express, and the most successful. The Roaring Twenties amplified the train's celebrity and gave birth to its legend. The Orient Express has enchanted artists, writers, spies, and adventurers as well—among the travelers seen on board were Lawrence of Arabia, Mata Hari, Marlene Dietrich, and Maria Callas, accommodated in high-luxury cabins, attending dances in lounge cars, and eating sophisticated lunches in the splendid dining cars.

Service did resume after the turmoil of the World War II, but the world was no longer the same. Europe's division into two blocs, the rapid spread of air travel, and the radically changed social climate, resulting firstly from reconstruction and the economic boom, and then from years of protest, led to a slow decline. The last **Paris – Istanbul tour** departed the French capital on May 19, 1977, and

the train, where travelers can meet each other, is the magnificent car No. 3674, where passengers can sip refined cocktails amid the sound of the ivories, with period music from the pianist each evening.

The three dining cars, named "Etolie du Nord," "Cote d'Azur," and "L'Oriental," are fabulous. Built between 1926 and 1929, they served for decades as part of CIWL's major European trains, and today they convey all the charm of those journeys, when travelers appeared for dinner in tuxedos and bejeweled ladies wore splendid evening dresses. Linen tablecloths, crystal glasses, and precious porcelain plates enhance the menus prepared by great chefs with international experience. Even today, lucky travelers follow a dress code, which changes depending on the time and the event attended.

No less luxurious or refined are the cabins, available in various configurations and sizes. They range from the Grand Suites, defined

arrived on the Bosphorus three days later, on May 22. An era was ending, but the legend lived on.

The **Venice Simplon Orient Express** is the original name of the train that from 1909 traveled the route through the Simplon tunnel to Venice, rather than heading north of the Alps toward Vienna. Today, it is no longer entrusted to the company's best steam locomotives, but it has again become a fantastic set of seventeen vintage coaches in elegant dark blue livery, embossed with the large golden CIWL logo. It has been completely restored in terms of the period's furnishings yet equipped with every comfort.

Coming aboard one of the cars is like traveling to a century ago: the interiors are lined with elegant panels inlaid with fine woods, accompanied by Lalique glass panels and wax decorations. Each table in the common areas is illuminated by an elegant abat-jour, and armchairs and sofas are upholstered in rich fabric. The heart of

64 top – The luxurious Grand Suite of the Orient Express takes passengers back to the exclusive rides of the early 1900s, traveling between major European capitals and seaside resorts on the Mediterranean.

64 bottom – One of the fine decorative glass panels produced in the 1930s by René Lalique and incorporated into the wood paneling of the dining car.

65 left – Wood paneling covers the walls of an Orient Express sleeping car compartment, displaying its impressive marquetry.

65 right – The stunning interior of the Orient Express lounge car, with sofas and armchairs.

To work on the Orient Express is the dream of many great international chefs. Among them is the French chef Jean Imbert, who has come up with a menu consisting of simple dishes made with fine ingredients: sea bass, poultry, lobster, and roasted turbot, all cooked to order in the train's kitchens (with the difficulties that entails). These delights are assigned to specific courses: an appetizer, two dishes of one's choice at lunchtime, and two dishes of one's choosing in the evening, cheese, and dessert. Of course, breakfast and afternoon tea are also supplied, as are snacks to be enjoyed at the bar. Knowing that the train runs from the end of March to the beginning of November, the chef plans to adjust the menu at least three times to make use of seasonal ingredients. Twelve cooks work on the train and are divided into three kitchens, which are fitted with the equipment necessary to serve 120 passengers at once.

without false modesty as "the epitome of luxury" with a large double bed, mirrors, and ornamental fittings, equipped with a private marble bathroom, to the suites with one or two beds, which turn into elegant private lounges during the day, decorated in an art deco style. There is no shortage of historic cabins, where a double sofa turns into luxurious bunk beds for the night.

The true star of the journey is the train itself, the Orient Express, with its **timeless carriages** and a life on board that projects passengers into a film where, for once, they are protagonists rather than spectators. For this reason, the Orient Express seems to overshadow the cities of departure and arrival where, again through Belmond, travelers can add a stay of one or two days to open and close the truly unique experience.

Of course, the Alpine crossing, the ascent toward the Brenner Pass, as well as the French countryside and the lagoon when arriving in Venice are all fantastic views to be enjoyed, all while being pampered by stewards on the train, in historic blue livery with golden trim. The success of this train has now multiplied the itineraries it offers, stopping in some of Italy's most beautiful historic cities and many European capitals.

66/67 – Elegant Orient Express coaches parade along the verdant Austrian Inn River valley near Roppen.

66 bottom – A panorama of Paris with the Eiffel Tower, with a gargoyle at the top of Notre Dame Cathedral in the foreground.

67 – Santa Lucia in Venice, the arrival station of the Orient Express, faces Venice's famous Grand Canal.

In addition to Venice, in Italy the train now stops in Rome, Florence, and Verona, while in the rest of Europe, connections are offered to—in addition to the historical Paris and London, and, of course, Istanbul—Amsterdam, Brussels, Geneva, Prague, Vienna, and Budapest as cities of departure or destination.

The Belmond website illustrates which routes are available each season with their travel dates, as well as their various service options, and the relative cost is, understandably, quite demanding. Cities change, routes change, but the legend of the Orient Express remains the same. It is a name and a symbol that have become part of the collective imagination, thanks in part to novels like Agatha Christie's *Murder on the Orient Express* and *Stamboul Train* by Graham Greene, and movies like *From Russia with Love*, with James Bond's escape set on this very train. Imagine being a secret agent, or detective, and imagine an adventure on the Orient Express.

Bergensbanen

On a journey from Oslo to Bergen, to discover the Norwegian landscape and impressive vistas en route to Flåm.

According to many travelers, the railroad line that connects Norway's two major cities, the capital of Oslo and Bergen, surrounded by mountains and fjords on the southwest coast of the country, is one of the most beautiful in the world, guaranteeing an unforgettable, emotional experience for travelers in both summer and in winter.

The **Oslo – Bergen railroad** (Bergensbanen or Bergen Line) is also Norway's main line—a standard-gauge, single track, 493 kilometers (306 miles) long. It travels some of the Scandinavian nation's most beautiful landscapes, from the countryside outside Oslo at sea level, climbing through forests and lakes, to Finse station with an elevation of over 1,222 meters (4,000 feet), the highest point of the entire route.

This part of the route crosses the Hardangervidda, the largest plateau of its kind in Europe, most of which is part of the unique and beautiful Hardangervidda National Park. The entire plateau is located above the tree line, where, due to elevation or latitude, trees are unable to grow. These are extremely ancient lands, and the landscape is characterized by bare moorland, punctuated by numerous ponds, lakes, rivers, and streams. The environment is inhospitable and wild, but one of intense beauty, which can be enjoyed from the train in complete safety and comfort.

After crossing the plateau, the train descends toward Bergen, offering views of fjords, waterfalls, and rivers.

The train stops at twenty-one stations between Oslo and Bergen. One of them is Myrdal, from which a short but singular, and spectacular, line branches off to Flåm, a small village at the apex of one of Norway's most beautiful fjords. It is a true masterpiece of rail engineering that is worth a visit in its own right, and it presents an opportunity to break up the journey from Oslo into two trips by spending the night in Flåm and continuing

68 – A small, colorful Bergensbanen station stands out against the snowy Hordaland landscape.

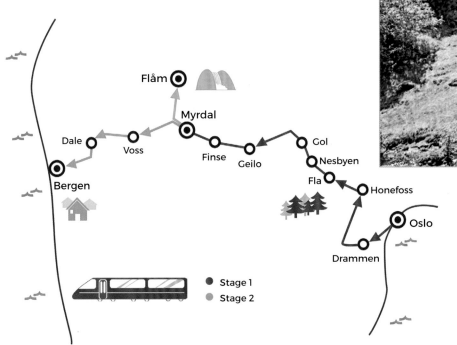

Departure: Oslo
Arrival: Bergen
Distance: 493 km (306 miles)
Duration: 7 hours
Stages: 2
Country: Norway

*68/69 – The historic Flåmsbana
is a very well-known railroad that
departs from Myrdal, descending
to the village of Flåm on the
Aurlandsfjord.*

PRACTICAL TIPS

THERE ARE THREE TO FOUR TRAINS PER DAY THAT TRAVEL THE ENTIRE LINE, WHOSE TIMETABLES MUST BE CHECKED ON THE VY (NORWEGIAN RAILWAYS) WEBSITE. TICKETS CAN ALSO BE PURCHASED ONLINE THERE. THE JOURNEY TAKES APPROXIMATELY SEVEN HOURS. TRAVELERS CAN PAY A LOWER PRICE BY BOOKING UP TO THREE MONTHS IN ADVANCE. FOR AN ADDITIONAL CHARGE, BIKES AND DOGS CAN BE BROUGHT ON BOARD. INTERRAIL PASS HOLDERS CAN GET A 30% DISCOUNT ON THE TICKET PRICE.

USEFUL WEBSITES
Norwegian railway: **https://www.vy.no/en**
Flåmsbana Railway:
https://www.visitnorway.it/listings/the-fl%C3%A5m-railway/4533
**https://norwaysbest.com/activities/flamsbana---the-flam
-railway/?referrer=4081**

the next day toward Bergen.

The Oslo – Bergen railroad line was built between 1875 and 1909, in very difficult environmental conditions due to the region's frigid and snowy winters. There are 182 tunnels dug into the rock for a total length of 73 kilometers (45 miles), and of these, ten are more than 2 kilometers (1.2 miles) long. Over the decades, the track has also undergone various adjustments to ensure reliable operation in all weather conditions. The line was electrified, beginning already in 1954 through 1964, and in 1992, the Finse Tunnel was inaugurated between Finse and Hallingskeid. This made it possible to avoid one of the open-air sections of track where it was more difficult to keep the train running in winter.

A trip on the Bergensbanen should be done twice: in the summer, to admire the colors of the moss and lichen on the plateau's barren expanses, and in wintertime, to experience the dramatic landscape and see how the train makes its way through the snow and ice. According to experienced travelers, to enjoy the most beautiful scenery, it is best to book a seat on the left side of the train heading from Oslo to Bergen and, of course, on the right side if you are traveling in the opposite direction. The carriages are modern and comfortable, and are equipped with WiFi, though the connection can be difficult in some cases, due to the many tunnels. Each train includes a buffet car, where passengers can sit and consume hot and cold dishes, snacks, coffee, and drinks while continuing to admire the landscape.

If you opt for a trip without intermediate stops, Oslo and Bergen of course offer many sight-seeing opportunities: in Oslo, in addition to the beautiful parks, the Munch Museum, dedicated to the artist who painted the famous *Scream*, and the National Gallery are worth seeing, but the Viking Ship Museum is equally interesting. Bergen, meanwhile, is a city surrounded by fjords and mountains. In addition to taking a cruise in the fjords, it is worthwhile visiting the fish market and the Bergenhus Fortress, or simply taking a stroll among the distinctive colored wooden houses in the historic center.

Time permitting, a trip on the Bergensbanen should include a stint discovering the **Flåm** Line. This short line departs from Myrdal station along the Oslo – Bergen line, at an elevation of 866 meters (2,841 feet), and on its journey of just 20 kilometers (about 12.5 miles) descends to 2 meters (about 6.5 feet) above sea level in Flåm, a village of fewer than 500 inhabitants, on the narrow Aurlandsfjord.

In addition to the beautiful landscape of the Flåm Valley, this line has technically fascinating features: the route is all slope, with some sections at **a gradient of 5.5%**. This is overcome, as the railway workers say, with **natural "adhesion,"** meaning that the trains do not use a rack between the rails to ensure the necessary grip when ascending and braking when descending. The number of railways in the world that overcome similar slopes without a rack can be counted on one hand.

If this weren't already an impressive feat, the path hand-dug between rocks and tunnels, with very tight curves and passages offering breathtaking views over the valley and down into the sea within the fjord, is unique.

The journey takes about an hour, at a maximum speed of 40 km/h (25 mph) including eight stops. The line was built between 1923 and 1940 to create a commercial link between towns along the Aurlandsfjord and the railway to Oslo and Bergen. It was electrified in 1944, one of the very first in Norway to undergo the transformation, retiring the steam locomotives that, until then, had ensured service. Until 1991, it also operated the local public transport service in connection with ferries from Flåm to Gudvangen. Then, the opening

70 – The splendid natural scenery surrounding the Bergensbanen is some of the most beautiful in all of Europe.

71 top – The charming Aurlandsfjord and the small town of Flåm at sunrise. This enchanting place serves as the Flåmsbana line's terminus.

71 center – Oslo's harbor is one of its great attractions. Set on the Oslofjord, it offers views of the sea and the city.

71 bottom – An aerial view of Bergen's old town.

*72/73 – A shot from the window of the train
descending from Myrdal to the town of Flåm along
the spectacular Flåmsbana railroad line.*

For some years, Norway has been experimenting with a new television genre, an unusual, "slow" television, which is enjoying great success with the public. The first program in the series was called "Bergensbanen – Minutt for Minutt," a direct train ride on the rail line connecting Bergen and Oslo, lasting seven hours and fourteen minutes. It was broadcast in 2009 by the public broadcaster NRK, garnering an average of 176,000 viewers and reaching 1.2 million viewers total (in a country that has five million inhabitants). The program simply broadcast the images coming from a single camera, placed in the cab of the locomotive next to the driver. There was no programme direction: just seven hours and fourteen minutes of landscape, stations, tunnels, and more landscape. There are no details yet on the success of the program that followed: eighteen hours of salmon swimming upstream.

of the new road to Bergen, with a consequent decrease in passengers and cessation of freight transport, meant the line risked closure. In 1998, the line's management was taken over by a local company, which, in collaboration with the Norwegian state railroad, turned it into a tourist line. Today, it is the third most popular destination in the country according to visitor numbers.

The train consists of six B3 **vintage coaches** with distinctive wooden interiors and painted a beautiful dark green, pulled by a modern El 18 locomotive. From May to September, there are about ten departures per day in each of its two directions, while in the winter months, the number of tours drops to four.

The train stops at each station for five minutes to allow passengers to get off and take photos. One of these stops is for Kjosfossen waterfall, one of the most beautiful in Norway.

In addition many activities are available in Flåm and its surroundings, from mountain biking or hiking to cruises in the fjords. From Vatnahalsen station visitors can reach the **Flåm Zipline**, an adrenaline-pumping descent hanging from a steel cable 1,381 meters (4,530 feet) long, during which one can easily reach 100 kilometers, or 62 miles, per hour. Those who prefer to not risk a heart attack can opt for a quiet (free) visit to the Flåmsbana Museum, which tells the story of the railway's construction and whose exhibits include an old El 9 electric locomotive.

73 top – One of the comfortable modern trains that travels the Bergensbanen between Oslo and Bergen each day.

73 bottom – Another image of the Flåmsbana, near the Flåm terminus.

Inlandsbanan

Nearly 1,300 kilometers (808 miles) from Kristinehamn to Gällivare: exploring the untamed landscape beyond the Arctic Circle and discovering Lapland.

The **Inlandsbanan**, literally the "inland line," is a railroad that travels across Sweden for 1,288 kilometers (nearly 800 miles) heading south to north. The route starts in Kristinehamn, about a three-hour drive north of Stockholm, then stops, in addition to many smaller towns, in Mora and Östersund, before arriving at its final stop, beyond the Arctic Circle: Gällivare, in Lapland. The railway is single-track and not electrified after the very first stretch north of Kristinehamn.

The wild landscape is dominated by birch forests, lakes, and small rivers, populated with an abundance of wildlife—including, of course, reindeer, who often move along the tracks in groups.

Open to traffic in 1937, the Inlandsbanan was designed to connect the country's inland towns in sparsely inhabited areas and encourage their development, and to provide a route that was better protected than the one along the coast in the event of conflict. In the 1960s a road was built parallel to the railway, and with the growth of car use, the Inlandsbanan became less important. There was a serious risk that the longest and most scenic stretch, from Mora to Gällivare, would close. In 1990, local communities began to organize to prevent this unhappy ending—the entire section, from Mora to its terminus in Lapland, was purchased by the territory's various municipalities with the establishment of Inlandsbanan AB, the company that

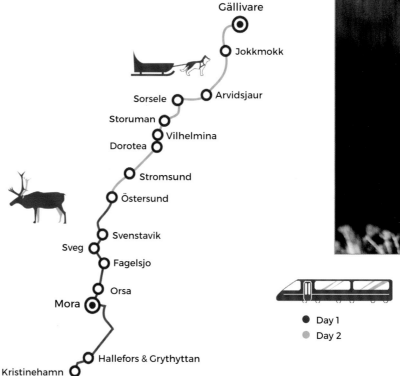

74 – The town of Jokkmokk is one of the last stops before the Gällivare terminus in northern Sweden.

Gällivare
Jokkmokk
Sorsele
Arvidsjaur
Storuman
Vilhelmina
Dorotea
Stromsund
Östersund
Svenstavik
Sveg
Fagelsjo
Orsa
Mora
Hallefors & Grythyttan
Kristinehamn

● Day 1
○ Day 2

Departure: Kristinehamn
Arrival: Gällivare
Distance: 1,288 km (800 miles)
Duration: 2 days
Stages: 2
Country: Sweden

74/75 – The railcar that provides summertime tourist service on the line, with its image reflected in the waters of Lake Tansjoborg, just north of the Orsa station.

PRACTICAL TIPS

FOR A MODEST SURCHARGE, PASSENGERS ARE ALLOWED A BICYCLE
ON BOARD THE TRAIN (RESERVING THE SEAT IN ADVANCE) OR A PET.
EACH SEAT HAS A USB OUTLET FOR CHARGING MOBILE PHONES
AND TABLETS. THERE IS ALSO A COMPLIMENTARY WIFI CONNECTION
AVAILABLE, THOUGH ITS SPEED MAY VARY DEPENDING ON THE PART
OF THE COUNTRY BEING TRAVELED. EACH TRAIN IS EQUIPPED WITH
A DEFIBRILLATOR. THE RANGE OF EXCURSION ACTIVITIES CAN BE
EXPANDED VIA THE REGION'S VARIOUS BUS SERVICES, WHICH ARE
CLEARLY MARKED IN EACH PLACE THE TRAIN STOPS.

USEFUL WEBSITES
Inlandsbanan:
https://res.inlandsbanan.se/en

The Tågab railroad company, which manages trains on the line's
Kristinehamn – Mora section:
https://www.tagakeriet.se

Arvidsjaur Tourist Office for the steam train:
arvidsjaurlappland@arvidsjaur.se

INTERESTING FACTS

Each year, the railway association Arvidsjaurs
Järnvägsförening organizes steam train tours along
the Inlandsbanan line from Arvidsjaur to Slagnäs, then
terminating at Lake Storavan. This historic train is comprised
not only of a steam locomotive but also of vintage railcars,
including a bar or restaurant car. It travels on Fridays and
Saturdays, with a departure in the late afternoon and return
to Arvidsjaur late evening. (in summer, the sun almost never
sets). In addition to the short stop in Slagnäs, where the
locomotive is disconnected and taken to the opposite end
of the train for its return, the train has a longer stop by a
beach on Lake Storavan. There, the bravest of passengers
can take a dip, while the majority can simply grill some food
outdoors. The distance between the two locations is about
60 kilometers (38 miles). Information and reservations are
available at the local tourist office.

*76 – Storstupet is a deep canyon along the Ämån River north of
Orsa. Here, the Inlandsbanan crosses the Ämån on a narrow
railroad bridge 34 meters (about 110 feet) above the river.*

still owns the line and manages it today.

The line's traffic is used exclusively for tourism, limited to the summer period from June to August, with trains between Mora and Gällivare running daily. Additional special trips are offered with the train ride as a comprehensive tourist package, lasting up to six days, including sights and excursions along the route, with stops in the most exciting locations. Some special trains are also available in winter and during the Christmas season. Certain tours also feature a vintage train pulled by a steam locomotive, while the daily service is carried out using comfortable diesel-powered railcars with bar service. A guide on board describes the areas traveled and recounts the history of the line.

Opportunities for travel on this magnificent route vary: passengers can opt for a full tourist package, or simply buy the train ticket and design their own itinerary. The latter approach is facilitated by an Inlandsbanan Card, which, in addition to other benefits, allows passengers to **"hop on / hop off"** while traveling in the Swedish hinterland. The pass offers two weeks of unlimited travel, allowing passengers to travel on the train, make excursions and go sightseeing, then continue onward to the next stop. Naturally, the Interrail pass is also accepted.

The full journey on the Inlandsbanan from Mora to Gällivare takes two days, and passengers must spend a night in Östersund. Just one train travels in each direction per day, departing at lunchtime from Mora and arriving, after traveling 321 kilometers (almost 200 miles), in Östersund in the evening, around 8:30 p.m. The stops at three stations along the way are fairly long, so travelers have time to explore the surrounding landscape.

The train departs early next morning from Östersund and reaches Gällivare some twelve hours later, just in time to admire the **midnight sun** between June 5 and 6, weather permitting.

At times, the train also stops for longer periods on this second day of travel, and passengers are able to exit the train. Many hours are then spent on board, but the journey is anything but boring, as the surrounding landscape is truly unique, and the guide on each train shares interesting anecdotes and information.

Among the most captivating stops is at Jokkmokk, where the railroad crosses the Arctic Circle. Travelers are advised to have some extra days to spare in order to fully enjoy locations along the railroad and learn more about the traditions and culture of Lapland's native populations.

One of these enaging spots is the Inlandsbanan Museum, occupying the old station building in Sorsele, which details the history of the line's construction.

The three towns of Mora, Östersund, and Gällivare each deserve at least a one-day stop. There travelers can discover, apart from the natural surroundings, the lifestyle of these northern region inhabitants, their culture, and their passions. The Inlandsbanan line is the best way to explore the lesser-known Sweden, proudly linked to its land and its most alluring traditions.

77 top – An overview of the city of Östersund, a popular tourist destination for winter sports.

77 bottom – A glimpse of Mora, a city known for hosting Vasaloppet, the oldest cross-country ski race in the world, and the departure station for trains on the Inlandsbanan.

Belmond British Pullman

Excursions from London to various British destinations featuring cathedrals, castles, vintage car racing and more on luxurious classic coaches.

The **Belmond British Pullman** is a tourist train that offers luxury two-day, weekend, and one-day trips to various destinations in the United Kingdom from London. One of the most popilar routes is to Canterbury. The train belongs to Belmond Management Ltd., a global operator in the tourism and travel sector. The company owns six luxury trains, the most famous of which is certainly the Orient Express. One of the British Pullman's tasks is to welcome and carry travelers on the Orient Express London – Paris – Venice route while they are on British soil: the Orient Express is not capable of travel on the island due to its Continental loading gauge, which is broader than the gauge adopted in the United Kingdom. However in terms of luxury and elegance, the British Pullman coaches fully match those of the Orient Express.

The travel philosophy on the British Pullman is simple yet sophisticated. It offers a trip lasting a day, or two days at most, to visit a significant location in Britain, to attend a sporting event, or to participate in one of the journey-events taking place entirely aboard the train, like its **Murder Mystery Lunch**. All tours begin and end at London's historic Victoria Station. A journey with the British Pullman is perhaps more important than the destination itself, thanks to its original carriages from the 1920s, which have been beautifully restored, bringing passengers back to the glory days of grand railroad journeys. Equally exclusive are the dishes and wines served on board in an elegant, sophisticated setting.

The train's original fittings, including the brass luggage racks, have been patiently restored, and period-appropriate elements have been added, such as table lamps and art deco armchairs. Coach interiors are clad in wood marquetry paneling restored by the family company A Dunn & Son, founded in 1895 and the original creator of some of the panels.

78 – A dining car on the Belmond British Pullman, richly decorated for a special Christmas journey.

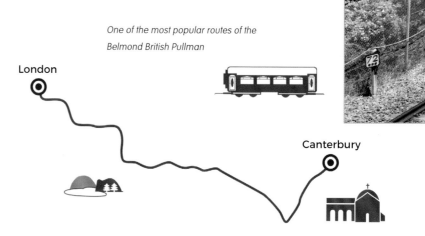

One of the most popular routes of the Belmond British Pullman

London

Canterbury

Departure: London
Arrival: Canterbury
Distance: 198 km (124 miles) – round trip
Duration: 8 hours
Stages: 1
Country: United Kingdom

*78/79 – The Belmond British
Pullman hauled by the splendid
"Clan Line" Merchant Navy Class
Pacific locomotive no. 35028
along the Kent coast on one of the
alternative tours.*

The eleven Pullman cars can accommodate up to 226 passengers around tables for one, two, or three people, but private compartments for four are also available.

Some of the carriages were part of the famous **Brighton Belle** train and reserved for travel by members of the royal family. Their history has been patiently reconstructed in detail, though related documents were lost in the Blitz during the Second World War.

In its typical configuration, the train is made up of fourteen carriages, eleven of which are historical (the rest being service cars) and is normally towed by a diesel locomotive with matching brown and cream paint. On special occasions, this locomotive is replaced by a steam-powered one.

Many destinations and events are offered, varying over time and according to the season, including the Great British Seaside: Hastings; a Luminary Champagne Afternoon Tea; Chatsworth House; Historic Bath by Steam; the Goodwood Revival; and Historic Canterbury. These range from a visit to the seaside to a journey of little more than two hours sampling special pastries with tea and champagne all while aboard the train, from an excursion to the Chatsworth House

*80 – The Belmond British Pullman's highly elegant vintage coaches,
pulled by a steam locomotive, take us back to the luxury train travel
of the early 1900s.*

81 top left – The Belmond British Pullman luxury tourist train on one of its many excursions, crossing the Stanway Viaduct near Toddington in Gloucestershire.

81 bottom left – Chatsworth House, destination of one of the Belmond British Pullman's excursions, is one of England's most famous and enchanting historic residences. It is home to the Duke and Duchess of Devonshire.

residence to taking a steam locomotive to Bath, or a tour to West Sussex to join the Goodwood Revival classic car race. In sum, any occasion could be a worthy excuse to travel on the Belmond British Pullman. One of its most popular – but infrequent – excursions is a day trip to explore Canterbury.

The Canterbury train leaves London's Victoria in the morning. Brunch with a Bellini is served on the outward journey as the train traverses southeast London and the Kent countryside. Upon arrival at Canterbury East, a walk will take passengers to the cathedral, where a brief choral performance is followed by optional guided tours of the historic building. Alternatively, one can walk freely around the city. The return journey departs from Canterbury West station and welcomes day-trippers back on board with a glass of chilled champagne while en route back to London, arriving in the early evening, followed by a three-course dinner accompanied by a half-bottle of wine. It is a luxury trip in the name of maximum comfort.

INTERESTING FACTS

The American film director Wes Anderson is a great train enthusiast, and it is no coincidence that *The Darjeeling Limited* is one of his best-known films. Belmond Ltd. asked Wes Anderson to reinvent the interiors of the British Pullman's twenty-six-seat Cygnus Carriage. As a train-lover and passionate admirer of craftsmanship, the director has managed to find a careful balance between the historic preservation of the art deco–style car and a modern interpretation of its design. The carriage is dedicated to the Greek god of balance, often represented as a swan. Its entire design is full of meticulous references to myth and legend, including the elaborate waves and swan featured in the marquetry, the ceiling's silver leaf, and the swan-shaped champagne coolers.

81 right – The magnificent Great Cloister of Canterbury Cathedral in Kent, one of the oldest and best-known churches in England.

SCOTLAND
FORT WILLIAM TO MALLAIG

Departure: Fort William
Arrival: Mallaig
Distance: 68 km (42 miles)
Duration: 4 hours (morning return), 6 hours (afternoon return)
Stages: 1
Country: United Kingdom

82/83 – Pulled by a steam locomotive, the Jacobite transits the famous Glenfinnan Viaduct on Scotland's West Highland Line between Fort William and Mallaig.

The Jacobite

Full steam ahead on the spectacular West Highland Line between Fort William and Mallaig, following the tracks that Harry Potter made famous.

The mountainous region of the Scottish Highlands, in the northwestern part of the United Kingdom, is considered one of the most scenic and fascinating regions in the whole of Europe. Sparsely inhabited, with few roads and villages, it boasts a breathtaking natural scenery.

A great way to explore the area is to take a train traveling the West Highland Line, departing from Glasgow. The railroad's final stop is in Mallaig, with a secondary branch ending in the town of Oban. The journey can be made riding ordinary trains but is especially enthralling for those who choose a steam train called the **"Jacobite."** This train operates a tourist service that runs very frequently in summer between the stations of Fort William and Mallaig. Mallaig is 264 kilometers (164 miles) from Glasgow, but the railroad's first section is shared with the route to Edinburgh.

The actual West Highland Line route begins at Crianlarich station, where the line to Oban also branches off. From there, one finds the journey's first curiosity, as the two routes, after 5 kilometers (around 3 miles), each stop at separate stations in the small village of Tyndrum, with 167 inhabitants in all. This Scottish village is therefore the smallest town in the UK served by more than one train station: the Upper Tyndrum, for Mallaig, and Tyndrum Lower, for Oban.

After Tyndrum, trains bound for Mallaig begin to climb toward the marshy plateau of Rannoch Moor and arrive at the small Corrour station, lost in the moor and unreachable by any public road. This is the highest point of the track, about 410 meters (1,345 feet) high. From here, the track begins its descent towards Loch Treig, a lake about 9 kilometers (5.5 miles) long, which the line follows along its eastern shore. There are no viable roads here either, and **the train is the only way to easily travel** to these unspoiled surroundings.

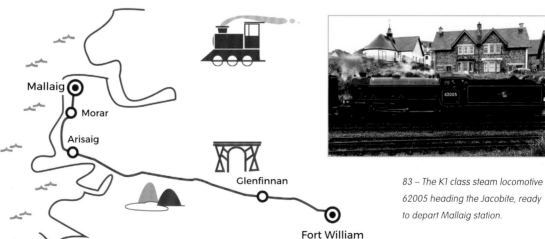

83 – The K1 class steam locomotive 62005 heading the Jacobite, ready to depart Mallaig station.

The train then arrives at Fort William and continues for about 20 kilometers (12.5 miles) before crossing the spectacular curved **Glenfinnan Viaduct.** The viaduct, all in stone, is now famous for its central role in a long steam train sequence in the first **Harry Potter** movie. After passing through Glenfinnan station, the line continues downhill for another 40 kilometers (25 miles) or so, crossing the town of Arisaig and offering a panoramic view of the Small Isles (which include Rum, the largest, Canna, Eigg, and Muck, and are part of the Inner Hebrides archipelago) until it stops at the town of Morar and finally reaches Mallaig.

The journey by regular train from Glasgow takes about five and a half hours to reach Mallaig, while from Fort William it takes about three hours and forty-five minutes. It might be a good idea, then, to dedicate more than a day to this line, traveling the first day with an ordinary train to Fort William and the next day exploring the remaining 68 kilometers (42 miles) to Mallaig and back on the Jacobite.

The train runs from Fort William to Mallaig every day from April to October of the week,

84 left – The remains of the famous Old Inverlochy Castle in Fort William. Few castles from the 1200s survive unaltered in Scotland today, and Inverlochy is one of the most complete.

84/85 – The Jacobite steam train leaves Fort William, here traveling below the storied Old Inverlochy Castle.

85 bottom – An aerial image of Loch Leven near Fort William illustrates the untamed beauty of the region traveled by the Jacobite.

Next to the famous viaduct at Glenfinnan station, you can visit a museum dedicated to the history of the West Highland Line. The indoor exhibit provides interesting facts and anecdotes about the remarkable Glenfinnan Viaduct and about life in the West Highlands, while the outdoor exhibits recount the story of the rural Scottish railway station over the past century. For those who wish to record or photograph the Jacobite as it travels the Glenfinnan Viaduct, which is absolutely stunning in its grandeur (universally known today, thanks to the Harry Potter movies), the approximate times are 10:58 a.m. outgoing and 3:00 p.m. return on the morning train, then 1:25 p.m. outgoing and 17:45 return on the afternoon train. The best place for photos can be reached by following the road under the large bridge then climbing up the hill to the left (west), where one can best appreciate the curve of the viaduct.

with a round trip in the morning, plus an afternoon round trip from May to September. Traveling with the Jacobite, the beauty of the landscape traveled is enhanced by all the charm of a journey from another time, riding in vintage cars drawn by a steam locomotive.

The line meanders a great deal, with substantial grades requiring the locomotive to utilize its full power, and the rhythmic snort of the locomotive under such stress acts as the soundtrack to the entire journey.

Some of the UK's most distinctive locomotives take turns pulling the train, including the K1 class 62005, dubbed the "Lord of the Isles" and some LMS Stanier Class 5MT locomotives, nicknamed

the **"Black Five"** because, unlike most British locomotives, they are painted completely black. These famous, extremely versatile machines have served in virtually every corner of Britain. The cars are also period pieces, all of the former **British Rail Mark 1** type from the 1960s; some are first-class lounge or compartment cars, while the rest of the train is made up of standard coaches from the same period. In all cars, the seats have upholstery with attractive designs and elegant tables with lighting. The train also includes a buffet car where tea, coffee, and various snacks are available. The journey is one step back in time, along the tracks of one of the most beautiful railroad lines in the world.

86/87 – Stanier Class 5 locomotive no. 44871 at the front of the Jacobite as it tackles the climb to Beasdale on a midsummer day.

88/89 – On an uninhabited stretch between Morar and Mallaig, the train appears almost lost in the landscape.

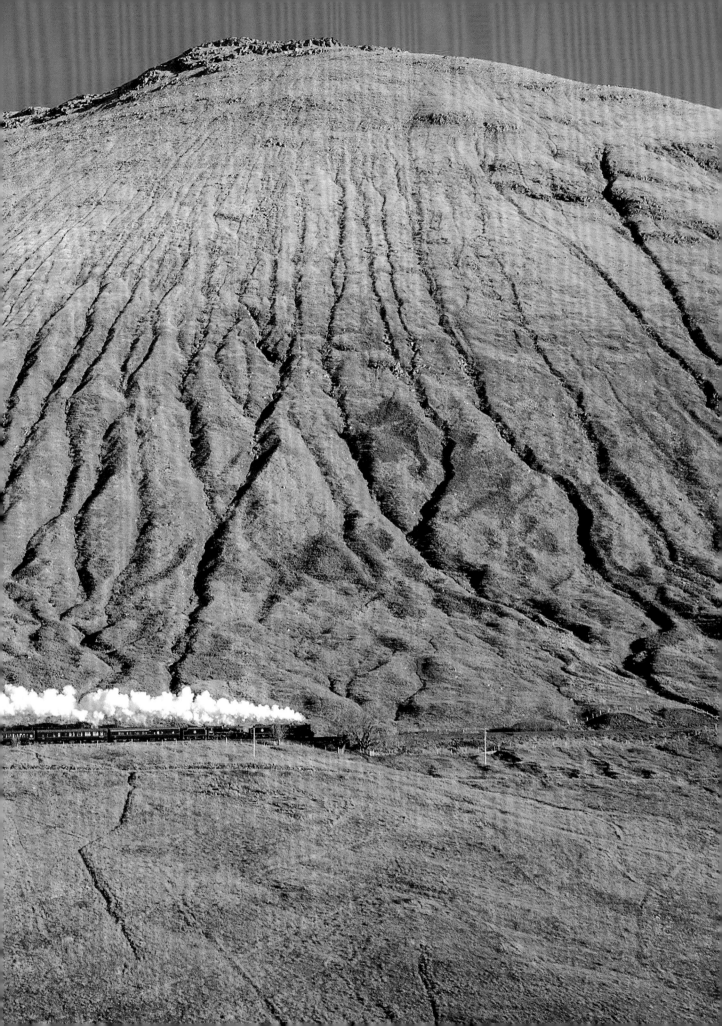

GERMANY

NORDHAUSEN TO WERNIGERODE
EISFELDER TALMÜHLE TO QUEDLINBURG
DREI ANNEN HOHNE TO BROCKEN

HARZQUERBAHN
Departure: Nordhausen
Arrival: Wernigerode

SELKETALBAHN
Departure: Eisfelder Talmühle
Arrival: Quedlinburg

BROCKENBAHN
Departure: Drei Annen Hohne
Arrival: Brocken

Distance: 141 km (87 miles) total
Duration: From 1 hour and 45 minutes to 4 hours and 10 minutes, according to route
Stages: 3, one per line
Country: Germany

90/91 – A train bound for the top of the Brocken advances through a fairy-tale landscape on a cold February morning.

Harzer Schmalspurbahnen

Discovering a railway network in Germany that takes travelers back to the golden age of steam locomotives.

The Harz is a region between Lower Saxony, Saxony-Anhalt, and Thuringia that marked the border between East and West Germany up until the fall of the Berlin Wall. Not only can passengers still ride a steam train there, but the experience is exhilarating. Due in part to the Cold War, this railroad, which plunges into the great forest of Harz Nature Park, extends across 25,000 hectares (61,780 acres) of woods and mountain ranges. Passing through small villages with their characteristic Germanic architecture reminiscent of **Brothers Grimm fairy tales**, the train remains "frozen" in the past. The 141 kilometers (88 miles) of narrow-gauge railroad, which were part of the German Democratic Republic's railroad network prior to unification, come exactly as they were at the end of the Second World War. The GDR (East Germany) did not have the resources to refurbish the railroad, especially given that it was a local, secondary network.

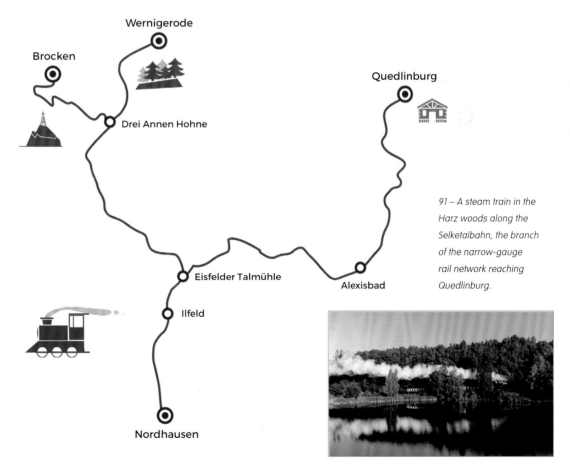

Wernigerode

Brocken

Drei Annen Hohne

Quedlinburg

Eisfelder Talmühle

Alexisbad

Ilfeld

Nordhausen

91 – A steam train in the Harz woods along the Selketalbahn, the branch of the narrow-gauge rail network reaching Quedlinburg.

PRACTICAL TIPS

TRAIN FREQUENCIES VARY, SO IT IS ADVISED TO CAREFULLY CONSULT TIMETABLES AND CHECK CONNECTIONS. JOURNEY DURATIONS ALSO VARY, FROM FOUR HOURS AND TEN MINUTES ON THE NORDHAUSEN-GERNRODE ROUTE TO TWO HOURS AND FIFTY MINUTES FROM NORDHAUSEN TO WERNIGERODE; FROM THIS STATION THE ASCENT TO THE BROCKEN TAKES ONE HOUR AND FORTY-FIVE MINUTES. TICKETS CAN ALSO BE PURCHASED ONLINE. DURING THE YEAR, IN ADDITION TO ORDINARY STEAM AND DIESEL TRAINS, THERE ARE ALSO TRAINS FOR SPECIAL OCCASIONS OR ANNIVERSARIES. INFORMATION IS ON THE RAILWAY SITE.

USEFUL WEBSITES
General information: **https://www.hsb-wr.de**
Summer timetables: **Sommerfahrpläne**
Winter timetables: **Winterfahrpläne**

So, the steam locomotives, train cars, and stations represent another era. Since the 1990s, these **Harzer Schmalspurbahnen** (Harz Narrow Gauge Railways) have grown into a formidable tourist attraction, so much so that the idea of replacing old trains with modern rolling stock was quickly ruled out.

There are three lines making up this network, all built at the end of the nineteenth century for local transport: the **Harzquerbahn**, or Harz Railway (Nordhausen – Eisfelder Talmühle – Drei Annen Hohne – Wernigerode); the **Selketalbahn**, the Selke Valley Railway (Nordhausen – Quedlinburg, with branches to Stiege and Hasselfelde or to Harzgerode); and the **Brockenbahn**, the Brocken Railway (Wernigerode – Drei Annen Hohne – Brocken). Each has its own distinct qualities, and even though tourists do ride the train in very large numbers today, the Harz Railway continues to carry out its ordinary public transport service. It is, therefore, a "real" railroad, and not only a tourist attraction.

The main attraction on the Harz line, along the 1-meter (3.3-foot) narrow-gauge tracks, are twenty-five steam locomotives. Some are stored or subject to periodic maintenance. Twelve massive class 99 five-axle tank locomotives built in the 1950s are generally in service, accompanied by three splendid, and certainly older, Mallet articulated steam locomotives. The Mallet 99 5902, in dark green livery, is actually from 1897, sharing, alongside its twin siblings the 5901 and 5903, the record of being the **oldest Mallet steam locomotive** operating in Germany. For trains intended primarily for local commuters, some fairly recent diesel railcars are also employed. Small diesel locomotives haul the service trains as well as some freight. Only on the

92 – The characteristic façades of period houses in Nordhausen's historic center.

93 left – The interior of the Harz Narrow Gauge Railway's historic T1 railcar. Built in 1933, the car has been back in service since the summer of 2021.

93 right – The fairy-tale castle of Wernigerode overlooking the small-town station, the terminus for a branch of the Harz Narrow Gauge Railway.

Brockenbahn do steam locomotives exclusively haul all the trains in circulation. The trains' maximum speed is 40 kilometers (about 25 miles) per hour, perfect for leaning out of windows to enjoy the local landscape and admiring the steam locomotive as it makes tight curves under load.

THE HARZQUERBAHN

The longest line on the Harz railroad connects the local area's two principal towns of Nordhausen and Wernigerode, stopping in about twenty smaller villages. The railway often **passes between houses**, almost as if it were a trolley line, its tracks lined by buildings that have preserved their medieval aesthetic, with colorful façades, sometimes frescos or traditional latticework. Traveling from Nordhausen, the train reaches Ilfeld, where the landscape becomes hilly and wooded, then continues on to the much-frequented Eisfelder Talmühle station, a Selketalbahn

branch point toward Quedlinburg. Meanwhile, the main line continues toward Wernigerode and faces a tough climb toward Benneckenstein station, which has a railroad museum worth visiting. The line for the Brocken breaks off at Drei Annen Hohne, while the Harzquerbahn route, on an especially **winding track**, heads toward Steinerne Renne through a dense forest. The journey comes to an end along a stream at Wernigerode Westerntor station, site of the railroad's workshops as well as the Wernigerode terminus.

This city has kept its medieval appearance intact and because of that has become an international attraction. Its quaint town hall, with its spires and small towers, has been selected by couples from around the globe for their marriage ceremonies. The castle boasts the same fantastic style and contains an entertaining museum.

94 left – The large hotel complex in the spa town of Alexisbad is over 200 years old and remained active until the 1990s.

94 right – Gernrode Abbey, founded in 959 CE, is the oldest Ottonian church in Germany.

THE SELKETALBAHN

Terminating at Quedlinburg, this line begins at Eisfelder Talmühle, from where the train route climbs toward a junction in Stiege. It then passes through small villages toward the town of Alexisbad, with its sixteenth-century castle and a prominent nineteenth-century spa, where today there is still no shortage of spas and luxury hotels. A short branch to Harzgerode also originates from this station. The main line instead continues onward to Mägdesprung, where there

are remnants of an ancient ironworks, founded in long-ago 1646 by Prince Frederick Albert of Anhalt-Bernburg.

The train continues its journey, stopping at Gernrode, site of the tenth-century church of Saint Cyriakus, the oldest Ottonian church in Germany, and finally reaches Quedlinburg. These last 8.5 kilometers (5 miles) of track between Gernrode and Quedlinburg are the only tracks that were constructed recently, inaugurated in 2006.

Since 1994, Quedlinburg has been included in UNESCO's list of World Heritage Sites, being a center of medieval and Renaissance culture. The new track was laid for a connection between the city and other UNESCO sites in Germany. Quedlinburg is undoubtedly the most beautiful historic town in the region, with its 1,400 fachwerkhäuser—centuries-old **half-timbered houses**—facing each other across the narrow streets of the historic center, where the magnificent Marktplatz sits. One must-see, a stone's throw from the square, is the small Schuhhof, the courtyard of the Shoemakers' Guild House, which has the same kind of two-paneled doors found in historic workshops.

INTERESTING FACTS

The summit of the Brocken, in addition to being the highest point of the Harz mountains and the arrival station of the steam train, is a place marked by history, at least that of the twentieth century. On this mountain, in 1935, the first television tower in the world was built, which functioned until the outbreak of the Second World War. Battered after the conflict, the summit found itself in the territory of the German Democratic Republic, and after the construction of the Berlin Wall in 1961, it was declared a high military security area. From the top, one could in fact easily spy on transmissions in West Germany. Border troops settled in the railway station, and both the Red Army and secret police took possession of the area. The entire top of the Brocken was surrounded by a reinforced concrete wall, made up of 2,318 sections, each weighing 2.4 tons and 3.6 meters (11.8 feet) high.

94/95 – An aerial view of Stiege Castle. It sits on the shore of the lake created by the Rappbode dam, near Oberharz am Brocken.

96/97 – The steam train departs from the top of the Brocken on a cold winter day, descending toward Drei Annen Hohne station.

96 – Winter in the Harz can be very cold and snowy, but the steam locomotives continue their daily service undeterred.

THE BROCKENBAHN

An ascent via the railroad departing from Drei Annen Hohne station on the Harzquerbahn to the top of the Brocken, the highest point of the entire Harz mountain range, takes travelers back to the times of the **Cold War**. It was no coincidence that the mountain's summit was used by the Soviets as a fortified area for the Stasi (East German secret police). Surveillance and the interception of radio signals were conducted there due to the peak's position on the border of West Germany, capable of monitoring the entire surrounding area.

Prior to the fall of the Berlin Wall, this area was considered strategic, and the Brockenbahn only carried freight traffic: the Brocken was part of a military exclusion zone, where civilians were not allowed.

Today, the long ascent through the woods up to the summit's 1,142-meter (about 3,745-foot) elevation leads to a large building with a café and restaurant housed in the old television tower building. This railway excursion is not to be missed in summer, but that is also true in winter, when the locomotive advances through the snow enveloped in huge swirls of white steam.

The Brocken, however, is also famous for the legends surrounding it—tales of witches and spirits. Goethe is said to have drawn inspiration from some of these stories for his **Faust**, which is partially set here. There are in fact several annual events taking inspiration from Goethe's work and characters.

97 – The powerful bulk of the steam locomotive stands out against the snowy landscape; in the background stands an old TV tower covered in ice.

98/99 – A marvelous winter image of the steam train ascending toward the top of the Brocken, towed by a DB 99 class locomotive.

Heritage Steam Trams

In the Netherlands, a few kilometers from Amsterdam, a timeless museum railroad relives the era of late-1800s steam-powered streetcars.

About 50 kilometers (30 miles) from Amsterdam, easily reachable by a Nederlandse Spoorwegen (Dutch Railways) train, the **heritage railroad between Hoorn and Medemblik** is a destination not to be forgotten on a trip to the Netherlands.

The railroad line is short, just about 20 kilometers (12 miles) long, but it has a troubled, intriguing history. Inaugurated on November 3, 1887, with a single track and standard gauge, the line was originally managed by the company Locaalspoorwegmaatschappij Hollands Noorderkwartier. Although the distance covered was short, it followed a rather circuitous route that, was designed to minimize the amount of land to be expropriated and keep construction costs low. Dedicated essentially to a local service like a streetcar's, its limitations soon surfaced. It was first closed to passenger service from January 1, 1936, until May 29, 1940, and after a brief seven-month reopening, it closed again to passengers on January 5, 1941, staying active for freight transport until the 1970s. It reopened for passenger trains in May 1968 for tourism, sooner than other European heritage lines. Now, thanks to the Museumstoomtram Hoorn Medemblik, a museum inside the Hoorn station that relates the history of the steam-powered streetcar lines, it is one of the foremost locations devoted to the history of the Dutch railroad.

The railroad-museum is made all the more appealing by the opportunity to continue the journey by sea after arriving in Medemblik. There, passengers can take the **historic ferry** connecting the railroad terminus to the city of Enkhuizen, just as they did in the mid-twentieth century.

100 – The small port of Hoorn, a refuge for old sailing ships, dominated by the historic tower of Hoofdtoren.

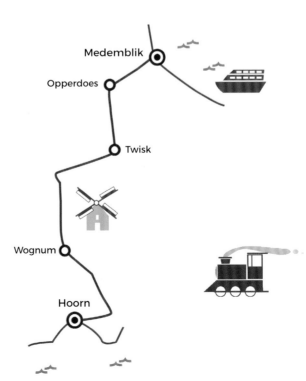

Departure: Hoorn
Arrival: Medemblik
Distance: 20 km (12.4 miles)
Duration: From 4 to 7 hours
Stages: 1 or 2 (train or train + ship)
Country: The Netherlands

100/101 – A small tram engine at the head of one of the historic trains that travel to Medemblik station from Hoorn.

102 top – The small steam-powered tram travels through the colorful Dutch countryside near Medemblik.

102 bottom – Once in Medemblik, the journey by steam tram can continue on board a vintage ferry to Enkhuizen.

103 – The magnificent "Bello" steam locomotive, no. 7742, ready to depart with its vintage train set from Medemblik station to Hoorn.

The ship used for this connection, the *Friesland*, is also vintage, built in 1955. In Enkhuizen, the ship docks near the Dutch Railways station, where it is easy to take a train back to Hoorn.

Wherever possible, the line's original stations have been restored to their old splendor: Wognum, Twisk, Opperdoes, and Medemblik are exactly as they were in the 1930s, while the Hoorn station has been rebuilt according to its original designs, including the working gas lamps in the square outside.

The locomotives, cars, and freight wagons that travel the line from Hoorn to Medemblik are diverse and highly interesting. The most well-known steam locomotive is the Nederlandse Spoorwegen 7742 "Bello," today the railway's only tank engine kept in running order. Built in 1914 in Berlin by Schwartzkopff, the small three-axle engine has traveled on many Dutch lines in its long history, bringing its career to a close on the streetcar line between Alkmaar and Bergen aan Zee.

The other steam locomotives in running order include three tramway engines, two of which are enclosed tram engines, which today are true rarities. The oldest is the no. 8 "Ooievaar" (or "Stork"), built in 1904, while the youngest is "only" from 1921. Equally fascinating are the **wooden streetcars** in the Hoorn – Medemblik trains: these bogie coaches are identical to those commonly used on all Dutch streetcar lines between 1890 and 1940, including first and second class with upholstered or wooden seats. Some of the trains also contain old enclosed freight cars.

The line is fully operational from April to September, but a reduced service is also offered in October and November. The timetable published on its website explains simply what travel opportunities are provided.

There are three options. The first is a round trip by train between Hoorn and Medemblik, which includes a visit to the Tram Museum, workshops in Hoorn, and the town of Medemblik with its historic harbor. The second and third combine the train journey between Hoorn and Medemblik with a ride to Enkhuizen on the old ferry. In this case, the journey can begin either from Hoorn or from Enkhuizen, and the transfer from train to ship always takes place in Medemblik. The ferry ride allows passengers to include a visit to the Zuiderzee Museum, dedicated to seafaring between the region's islands. The number of trains in service each day is greater during the high tourist season, offering visitors more possibilities to organize their own excursions.

PRACTICAL TIPS

ON EACH DAY OF OPERATION (IN YELLOW IN THE ONLINE TIMETABLE), A STREETCAR DEPARTS HOORN AND THE FERRY DEPARTS ENKHUIZEN AT THE SAME TIME IN THE MORNING. IN THE HIGH SEASON, MORE TRAMS ARE IN OPERATION.

USEFUL WEBSITES
The railroad:
Museum Stoomtram Hoorn-Medemblik https://www.stoomtram.nl

INTERESTING FACTS

The former *Friesland* ferry is registered as a national monument in the Dutch National Register of Sailing Monuments under the number 2500. The shipyard P. de Vries Lentsch, in the city of Alphen aan den Rijn, was commissioned by the Doeksen shipping company to build the ship, which is 52 meters (about 170 feet) long. Its launch took place in December 1955. The *Friesland* operated the ferry service between Harlingen and the island of Terschelling from 1956 to 1988. When a new *Friesland* entered service in the late 1980s, the ship was sold. Rederij Gebhard then used it for round trips on the Oosterschelde, and the ship had a permanent mooring based in Zierikzee. The ship has been used on the Enkhuizen – Medemblik route since 2002, in connection with the steam-powered streetcar run by the Hoorn – Medemblik Museum.

Rhaetian Railway

Up and down Alpine peaks in the Swiss Canton of Grisons, aboard the Rhaetian Railway's spectacular red trains.

Switzerland is, without a doubt, a paradise for lovers of train travel. And, if there is a special spot within this paradise, the **Rhaetian Railway** is there. Some of the most spectacular railroad routes in the world form part of its network, both public and tourist transport services are managed extremely efficiently, and the panoramic views of the mountains and towns at the bottom of the valley are compelling.

A trip to the Canton of Grisons to discover the extensive Rhaetian Railway, with its red trains traveling throughout the valleys and climbing up to the Ospizio Bernina station's 2,253-meter (7,392-foot) elevation, is an unforgettable experience. This is true even without boarding the **Bernina Express** or **Glacier Express**, the railway's two most famous trains.

The Rhaetian Railway manages a network of approximately 385 kilometers (239 miles), all with a narrow gauge of 1 meter (3.3 feet) and completely electrified at 11 kV AC, excluding the 61 kilometers (38 miles) of the Tirano – St. Moritz line, powered at 1000V DC. The railway mainly carries out local and regional public transportation services in the Canton of Grisons. Several routes are popular with tourists, but the railway also provides specific tourist trains, namely the Bernina Express and Glacier Express.

For an idea of the challenges encountered in building the various lines that make up the network, one need only recall that 84 tunnels were excavated (the Vereina Tunnel, at 19 kilometers, or 12 miles, is the longest in the world for a narrow-gauge railway), with 383 bridges and viaducts constructed. The grade on the network is often 4.5%, but the Bernina line reaches an incredible **grade of 7%**, without the use of a rack.

Construction of the railway began in 1888 with the route between Landquart and Davos, where its first steam trains circulated, then adding sections toward St. Moritz, Disentis, and Scuol-Tarasp.

BERNINA EXPRESS
Departure: Tirano
Arrival: St. Moritz
Distance: 61 km (38 miles)
Duration: 2 hours and 30 minutes
Stages: 1
Country: Italy Switzerland

GLACIER EXPRESS
Departure: St. Moritz
Arrival: Zermatt
Distance: 291 km (180 miles)
Duration: 7 hours and 30 minutes
Stages: 1
Country: Switzerland

104 – A spectacular aerial shot of the 126-meter-long (413-foot-long) Landwasser Viaduct along the Albula line, which, together with the Bernina line, has been declared a UNESCO World Heritage Site.

RHAETIAN RAILWAY
Total extension: 385 km (239 miles)
Stations: 102
Lines: 10
Highest point: Ospizio Bernina, 2,253 meters (7,392 feet)
Net height: Over 30% above 1,500 meters (4,921 feet)
Area served: Canton of Grisons

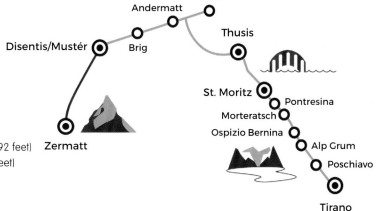

PRACTICAL TIPS

THE GLACIER EXPRESS RUNS THROUGHOUT THE YEAR, APART
FROM A SHORT BREAK BETWEEN MID-OCTOBER AND EARLY
DECEMBER. THE INTERRAIL PASS IS NOW VALID FOR ALL RHAETIAN
RAILWAY TRAINS, AND ON THE MATTERHORN GOTTHARD BAHN,
WHICH FORMS PART OF THE GLACIER EXPRESS ROUTE. THE
HOURLY LOCAL TRAINS BETWEEN CHUR, ST. MORITZ, AND TIRANO
CONSIST OF MODERN ALLEGRA ELECTRIC RAILCAR TRAINS WITH
ORDINARY COACHES (WHICH ARE NOT PANORAMIC BUT HAVE
WINDOWS THAT CAN BE OPENED).

USEFUL WEBSITES
Glacier Express: **https://www.glacierexpress.ch**

Bernina Express:
https://www.rhb.ch/it/treni-panoramici/bernina-express

Rhaetian Railway: **www.rhb.ch**

Thanks to its merger with Arosa and Bernina railways, the network expanded. Nearly the entire Rhaetian Railway network was completed just twenty-five years later. The most recent extension of the route, the Vereina Tunnel, was inaugurated in 1999. The latest event to boost the Rhaetian Railway's celebrity was its Albula and Bernina lines' adoption into the UNESCO list of World Heritage Sites on July 7, 2008, as "technically innovative examples of the development of the high alpine landscape and among the most spectacular narrow-gauge railways in the world." Only three other railway lines are included in the UNESCO list, in India, Austria, and, most recently, Iran.

The Albula line, from Thusis to St. Moritz, and the Bernina line, from Tirano to St. Moritz, are covered respectively by the Glacier Express (which departs from St. Moritz and arrives in Zermatt, outside the Rhaetian Railway network) and Bernina

Express tourist trains, but both lines can also be traveled aboard the standard local service trains provided by Rhaetian.

Let us explore the most beautiful and impressive points of these two lines, and the celebrated Bernina and Glacier Express tourist trains. The Bernina Express runs along the 61-kilometer (38-mile) length of line sharing its name, starting from Tirano station, in Italian territory. The journey begins, quite unusually, with the train traveling across the Piazza della Basilica **as if it were a streetcar,** then crossing the border and entering Val Poschiavo. After traveling a few kilometers, the train winds around itself, climbing the Brusio **spiral viaduct**, allowing it to gain altitude in a shorter space, and continues on toward Poschiavo. The train then takes the Cadera Tunnel and begins a very steep ascent up the track, with grades of

106 – The Bernina Express taking the famous Brusio spiral viaduct. Inaugurated in 1908, the viaduct is a UNESCO World Heritage Site, along with the entire Bernina line.

107 left – Ospizio Bernina, on the Bernina line, is the highest railroad station of the Rhaetian Railway at an altitude of 2,253 meters (about 7,390 feet).

107 top right – These modern, comfortable panoramic coaches on the Bernina Express allow passengers to fully enjoy the superb Alpine landscape.

107 bottom right – The Bernina Express runs alongside Lago Bianco, one of the three lakes found in the Bernina Pass.

up to 7% and repeated 180-degree bends, tunnels, and bridges set among the dense woods.

One of the most scenic parts of the route leads, within the space of a few miles, from a 962-meter (3,156-foot) elevation in Poschiavo to the Ospizio Bernina station at 2,253 meters (7,392 feet), the highest point of the line, and of the entire Rhaetian Railway. At this height, the landscape is very bare, and the railroad runs along the edge of the Lago Bianco. A few miles on lies the Morteratsch stop. The Morteratsch Glacier lies in front of the train, but, while the first tourists who stopped here in 1908 needed only to walk 150 meters (about 500 feet) to reach the edge of its ice tongue, today, due to climate change and the melting of the alpine glaciers, it is now a walk 3 kilometers (about 2 miles) long.

From there, the line descends more gently toward St. Moritz, first stopping at Pontresina, at the mouth of Val Roseg, then Celerina, its last stop before the famous town of St. Moritz.

All lines are also traveled by ordinary non-tourist trains. The Bernina Express train consists of coaches with domed windows, which cannot be opened, giving a broad view of the surrounding landscape, and in the summer, passengers can travel in uncovered panoramic coaches. There is a bar service on board. The Glacier Express is also made up of panoramic coaches. There are no open cars, but service offers catering, with hot dishes served at one's seat. First- and second-class tickets are available for both trains, and reservations are recommended. The Glacier Express also offers Excellence Class, which provides access to a special panoramic coach with much more space per passenger, along with other benefits.

108 – The Bernina Express near Pontresina, with the Bernina Range behind.

Here passengers can extend the journey by riding one of the Rhaetian Railway's many other trains, heading for Scuol-Tarasp or, opting for the 62-kilometer (39-mile) Albula line instead, traveling toward Thusis and then deciding whether to turn east toward Chur or west toward Disentis/Mustér. This latter route is that of the Glacier Express, the other famous **"red train"** of the Rhaetian Railway. It is also jokingly called **"the slowest express train in the world"** since, in order to cover the 291 kilometers (180 miles) between St. Moritz and Zermatt in the Canton of Valais at the foot of the Matterhorn, it takes about seven and a half hours.

The Glacier Express leaves St. Moritz station and heads toward Spinas station at the southern entrance of the 5.8-kilometer (3.6-mile) Albula Tunnel, which has been in service since 1903, reaching its highest point at an altitude of 1,820 meters (5,971 feet). After almost 120 years of activity, the old tunnel, excavated in unstable rock, is in need of renovation. However, the possibility of closing the line, one of the busiest in the network, was rejected in favor of excavating a new parallel tunnel, which is now almost complete.

Once out of the tunnel, the train begins its steep descent toward Thusis, 1,100 meters (3,609 feet) below the top of the tunnel. This

difference in elevation is overcome within the space of a few miles thanks to the **spiral tunnels** between Bergün and Preda, the Solis Viaduct, and the famed **Landwasser Viaduct**. This very high, curved masonry viaduct astounds for its elegance and for its abutment on a high cliff, which the train enters directly via a tunnel.

After Thusis, the train arrives at the branch station of Reichenau-Tamins and turns toward the city of Chur. There, the train reverses, running along the entire line toward Disentis/Mustér, where the Rhaetian Railway network ends. The train's coaches are attached to a locomotive from the Matterhorn Gotthard Bahn, a company born of a 2003 merger between the Furka Oberalp Railway and the Brig-Visp-Zermatt-Bahn, which handled the last leg of the journey.

The Glacier Express then crosses the Oberalp Pass at a 2,033-meter (6,670-foot) elevation, and continues via the long Furka Base Tunnel. It travels to the Oberwald station, once, but no longer, the place of departure for the old line that climbed the Furka Pass. The journey then continues toward Brig, where the coaches travel almost completely via **rack and pinion** for the last 44 kilometers (27 miles), finally leading the Glacier Express up to a 1,604-meter (5,300-feet) elevation at Zermatt station.

109 top – The Glacier Express crosses Tujetsch Viaduct near Sedrun.

109 bottom – A comfortable modern Glacier Express coach parked at St. Moritz station.

El Transcantábrico

A luxury trip along the northern Spanish coast, from San Sebastián to Santiago de Compostela.

Traveling by train in the first decades of the last century was synonymous with comfort and enjoyment. There were certainly a number of luxury trains that connected the European capitals or were bound for fashionable tourist destinations like the Côte d'Azur.

On board **El Transcantábrico**, travelers can discover the most remote cities and corners of northern Spain as they take in the Belle Époque atmosphere. It is the Spanish tourist train par excellence, offering a luxury journey from the city of San Sebastián to Santiago de Compostela. It takes lucky passengers on an eight-day tour, immersed in the romantic atmosphere of the early twentieth century, yet with all modern comforts. The actual train route, however, does not connect with the cities at the beginning and end of the overall journey: the train actually departs from Bilbao rather than San Sebastián and arrives at Ferrol station instead of Santiago de Compostela; these two short sections of the journey are covered by luxury buses.

El Transcantábrico travels over 500 kilometers (310 miles) on the narrow-gauge meter track belonging to FEVE (Ferrocarriles Españoles de Vía Estrecha), following the entire length of the northern, and very green, coast of Spain. A company was established in 1965 to simplify the set of operators managing various sections of its network (which extends 1,192 kilometers, over 740 miles), and since 2013 it has been incorporated into Renfe Operadora, the Spanish national railway network. It still maintains operational autonomy, today adopting the name of Renfe-Feve.

110 – Luxurious sofas in a lounge car of the tourist train El Transcantábrico.

- Day 1
- Day 2
- Day 3
- Day 4
- Day 5
- Day 6
- Day 7
- Day 8

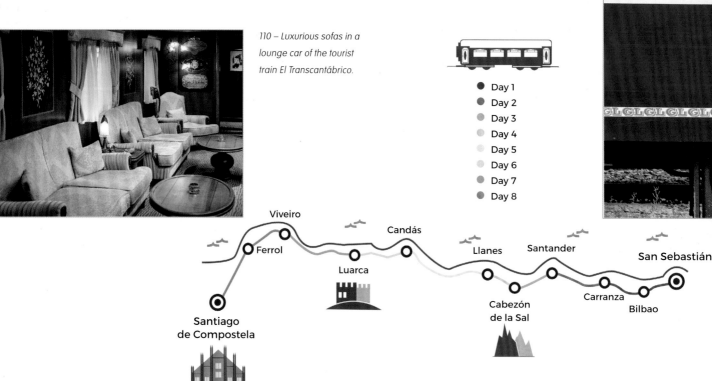

Departure: San Sebastián
Arrival: Santiago de Compostela
Distance: 904 km (562 miles)
Duration: 8 days
Stages: 8
Country: Spain

110/111 – A coach of El
Transcantábrico allows a glimpse
of the sophisticated interior of this
luxury train, which runs parallel to
the northern Spanish coast.

112 top – An aerial view of Alderdi Eder park, the town hall, and the castle on the hill of Urgull in San Sebastián.

112 center – The village of La Hermida shares a name with La Hermida Gorge, one of the natural wonders of the Picos de Europa mountain range.

112 bottom – El Transcantábrico traveling between the towns of Unquera and Cabezón de la Sal.

For twenty-five years, El Transcantábrico's tourist service has traveled across Cantabria, Castile, and Asturias, between the ocean and the marvelous Picos de Europa, the mountain range along the northern coast of Spain. The train, in its quiet saunter between Bilbao and Ferrol, offers glimpses of the Bay of Biscay. These alternate with views of the mountain range, which is largely part of the Picos de Europa National Park, making the journey all the more satisfying and engaging.

It is a fantastic way to travel, especially since this luxury tourist train offers travelers recently refurbished **vintage coaches**, which, while keeping the interiors intact, guarantee every comfort. The double suites with double or single beds, a private bathroom, a television screen, a computer, and adjustable air-conditioning are transformed during the day into comfortable lounges with large windows from which to admire the landscape.

Lunches and dinners are served in a luxurious dining car, while the four elegant lounge cars, original and specially **restored 1923 Pullman cars**, allow passengers to spend time in the company of other travelers. Musical events, parties, and shows are also organized in these spaces each evening. Following the evening entertainment, in order to ensure a peaceful rest—and to not miss a single mile of the wonderful landscape it traverses—the train is kept at the station through the night.

Yet each day, when the train makes a stop, a luxury coach awaits passengers, taking them to visit the many points of interest linked to the history and culture of northern Spain, accompanied by highly experienced guides.

The train departs from San Sebastián, where travelers meet at the Hotel Maria Cristina for a guided tour of the city and for lunch. This seaside resort is full of interesting sites, including the Old Quarter with its historic buildings, the beach, and iron sculptures by Eduardo Chillida emerging from the sea. In the afternoon, a luxury coach transfers passengers to Bilbao station, where they can board the train. This is where the actual railway journey begins, the first day ending in Carranza for an overnight stop.

On the second day, as breakfast is served, the train returns to Bilbao, where a first excursion is scheduled to visit the **Guggenheim Museum**. Lunch is served on the train en route to the city of Santander, deemed one of the most beautiful in all of Spain. Here travelers have the opportunity to visit the city before

and after dinner, which, of course, is served on board.

At night, the train remains stationary in Santander, then the next morning, on the third day of the tour, it runs to Unquera during the scheduled breakfast time. From there, passengers are taken by bus to La Hermida Pass, a wild gorge 21 kilometers (13 miles) long, and a conservation area for birds, where golden eagles can still be admired in flight. The excursion continues in the historic town of Potes, dominated by the Torre del Infantado ("tower of the infantry") with the medieval architecture and bridges from which it takes its name. Before lunch and the journey to El Capricho in Comillas, a fantastic nineteenth-century villa designed by Antoni Gaudí, travelers can experience the thermal baths of the Balneario La Hermida. Back on board, the journey continues to Cabezón de la Sal, where the train stops for the night.

The fourth day of the tour begins with a visit to the medieval city of Santillana del Mar, with its cobbled streets and historic district. It then continues to Altamira to see the museum dedicated to its famous Upper Paleolithic rock paintings. In the afternoon, passengers return to the train, and the journey continues to Llanes, where they dine and spend the night.

PRACTICAL TIPS

THE TRIP ON EL TRANSCANTÁBRICO CAN BE MADE EITHER FROM SAN SEBASTIÁN TO SANTIAGO DE COMPOSTELA OR IN THE OPPOSITE DIRECTION. THERE IS NO STRICT DRESS CODE ON THE TRAIN, BUT CLOTHING SUITED TO THE TRAIN'S ELEGANT ATMOSPHERE IS APPRECIATED. ADEQUATE CLOTHING AND COMFORTABLE SHOES ARE RECOMMENDED FOR PARTICIPATION IN OFF-TRAIN EXCURSIONS.

USEFUL WEBSITES
El Transcantábrico:
https://eltrentranscantabrico.com/en/the-train

Renfe-Feve:
https://www.renfe.com/es/en/suburban/cercanias-feve

113 – The Ribera Market in the center of Bilbao, where one can buy fresh fruit and vegetables or eat delicious pintxos at the small bars inside.

114 top – A glimpse of the medieval village of Potes, with its hanging houses and the river Deva.

The journey now on its fifth day, the train leaves Llanes for Arriondas. There, passengers make an excursion by bus to the Picos de Europa National Park, with a visit to the two lakes of Covadonga and the Covadonga Sanctuary, a sacred place rich in tradition and legend. Passengers are scheduled to return to the train for lunch while en route to Oviedo, capital of the Principality of Asturias. Oviedo is also the heart of pre-Romanesque Asturias, featuring treasures like the church of San Julián de los Prados. A visit to the city is planned here, then a return to the train, bound for Candás.

The sixth day begins with an excursion to the historic city of Avilés and then to Gijon with its beautiful beaches, archaeological remains, and Roman walls. After lunch, the train journey continues in the afternoon to Luarca, known as the villa blanca de la costa verde ("the white village of the green coast"), a little fishing village typical of the area, featuring the eighteenth-century house of the Marquises of Gamoneda and the church of Santa Eulalia. Here the

train makes its usual overnight stop.

On the penultimate day of this incredible ride, the train first comes to Ribadeo, where the day's first off-train excursion is planned. Then, during an onboard lunch, the train travels to the beautiful medieval city of Viveiro for a guided tour before dinner. This is the last night spent with the train.

The next day, it arrives in Ferrol, where the FEVE railway network sadly ends. Passengers must then say goodbye to the splendid set of cars that have pampered them for a week, then board the bus taking them to Santiago de Compostela. No one can turn down the chance to discover the famous cathedral there, still the final destination for pilgrims walking the **Camino de Santiago**. This dream of a trip is now complete. The same itinerary, without the luxury and excursions promised by El Transcantábrico, can be made traveling on ordinary FEVE trains, in a manner that is slightly more adventurous but, of course, much more affordable.

INTERESTING FACTS

You can also travel on the same line as El Transcantábrico riding Renfe-Feve regional trains from Bilbao in the Basque Country to Ferrol in Galicia. The train ride takes about nineteen hours from start to finish. Of course, one need not make the entire journey in one go, and it would be difficult to do so with timetable restrictions and train connections. There are more than one hundred stops along the way, including small villages with rural guesthouses where travelers can stay overnight. The duration of the journey depends on the number of stops, but, on average, it can take about a week to complete the journey between the two cities. It is best to book train tickets as you go, carefully checking the routes and timetables online or in-person at the stations. Individual tickets can be purchased each morning for a specific destination.

114 bottom – Beaches and cliffs follow one another near the town of Comillas.

115 – The famous Cathedral of Santiago de Compostela, in the city where El Transcantábrico's tour ends.

Linha do Douro

From Porto to Pocinho along the Douro River Valley, amid Port vineyards, azulejos, and intriguing local legends.

This railroad line largely follows the Douro River Valley eastward from Porto, nearly to the Spanish border, allowing passengers to admire some of northern Portugal's most beautiful natural scenery as they go past the terraced vineyards of the region, which produce Portugal's famous fortified Port wine. The line also connects two locations included in the UNESCO list of World Heritage Sites, Porto's historic center and the Alto Douro wine region. This railroad, which the Portuguese simply call the **Linha do Douro** ("Douro Line"), and especially a part of the route directed inland between Régua, Pinhão, and Pocinho, is considered one of the most beautiful in Europe. A day may suffice for a journey exploring these tracks and this valley, starting from Porto, Portugal's second city.

The line, built and then opened to traffic for added sections between 1875 and 1887, is 160 kilometers (nearly 100 miles) long and has a 1,668-millimeter-wide gauge (about 5.5 feet wide, the standard being 1,435 millimeters, or 4.7 feet); this is known as the **"Iberian gauge,"** since it was also adopted by the Spanish railways (apart from new high-speed lines). Its journey begins in Porto's monumental São Bento station, sharing the line, here double-track and electrified at 25 kV AC, with the Linha do Minho toward Valença until it reaches Ermesinde station. From this point on, the railroad bends sharply to the east until, after about 7 kilometers (nearly 4.25 miles), it reaches Valongo, where the line becomes a single track. It is, however, still electrified at 25 kV AC prior to reaching the station at Marco de Canaveses, about 60 kilometers (nearly 40 miles) from Porto.

116 – A characteristic Portuguese train in the Douro Valley: vineyards grow in the background, with grapes that will be used to create the valley's characteristic Port wine.

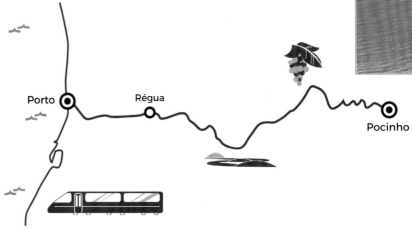

Porto   Régua   Pocinho

Departure: Porto
Arrival: Pocinho
Distance: 160 km (99 miles)
Duration: 3 hours and 30 minutes
Stages: 2
Country: Portugal

116/117 – A single image showing the two best ways one can explore the Douro Valley: by train and by riverboat.

There are many stories, real and fictional, told in the Douro Valley. One even has to do with the railroad, or rather with Dona Antónia Ferreira, nicknamed "Ferreirinha," the greatest wine producer of her time, who financed the construction of the line. Though very rich, she was also attentive to the needs of her people and was very well liked. According to legend, Ferreira was on a boat with the Baron of Forrester in the summer of 1861 when the boat began to sink. "Ferreirinha" was saved thanks to her ballooning skirts, which allowed her to float to the bank of the Douro. The Baron of Forrester, on the other hand, was dragged downward to the bottom of the river by the belt that he wore, laden with pounds of gold.

118 top – The small civil parish of Pinhão, whose tributary (the Pinhão River), flows into the Douro.

118 bottom – The beautiful Pinhão train station, whose exterior is decorated in traditional azulejo tilework.

The line once connected with the Spanish railroad toward Salamanca. This railroad closed its section that stopped at the Portuguese border in 1984, and the Portuguese railways were forced to limit service in 1988 to the station at Pocinho.

The rolling stock in daily use for its passenger service consists of Class 1400 diesel-electric locomotives and Class 592 railcars. These are all second-class trains, and some have no air-conditioning, yet this allows for windows to be opened, and, thanks to their modest speed, travelers can take wonderful photographs of the valley and the Douro.

There are several outbound and return trains, so travelers can "break up" their journeys and see at least some sights along the way. The stations themselves are especially interesting and well-kept, including Pinhão station, which is decorated with stunning azulejos—ornamental ceramic tilework, characteristic of Portuguese and Spanish architecture, which is decorated and glazed, very often using shades of cobalt blue. Another interesting stop is the town of Peso de Régua (its station simply named Régua) on the Douro River, where, in an older part of town, some small local restaurants can still be found. Also along the river is the Museu do Douro, which, in addition to relating the history of the valley and its famous wine, has temporary exhibitions of outstanding contemporary painters. Régua is also a major stopover location for cruises on the Douro River, and an entertaining option may be to travel part of the valley by boat before returning to the train at Pinhão, for example.

The journey continues toward the small town of Pocinho, where the line ends. Here the Linha do Sabor, a small, one-meter narrow-gauge railway, ran on magnificent articulated Mallet steam locomotives up until the mid-1980s, reaching Miranda do Douro.

Those fond of historical trains do, however, have an opportunity to travel on the steam train traveling between Régua and Tua from June to October. The journey is relatively short, normally taking an afternoon to make a round trip, but it is exceptionally scenic, combining passengers' experience of a vintage train with the opportunity to view the impressive landscape along the Douro. The train is made up of five **wooden vintage two-axle cars** with terraces at each end and pulled by the steam locomotive CP 0186, a tank locomotive dating to 1925. At the station, visitors can also observe maneuvers as the **locomotive is turned via a turntable** and its water is refilled, which is always an interesting sight. Otherwise, they can visit a wine house at the Pinhão station or discover local products from the area in Tua.

PRACTICAL TIPS

THE ENTIRE JOURNEY FROM PORTO TO POCINHO HAS A MAXIMUM DURATION OF ABOUT THREE AND A HALF HOURS, BUT THERE ARE TRAINS THAT MAKE DIFFERENT STOPS, AND IT IS A GOOD IDEA TO CHECK TIMETABLES AND STOPS ON THE WEBSITE FOR PORTUGUESE RAILWAYS (CP, COMBOIOS DE PORTUGAL).

USEFUL WEBSITES
Portuguese Railways: **https://www.cp.pt/passageiros/en**

The historic steam train:
https://www.cp.pt/passageiros/en/how-to-travel/For-leisure /Nature-and-Culture/douro-historical-train

For boat trips along the Douro River:
https://www.getyourguide.it/valle-del-douro-l4965/crociere-e -tour-in-barca-tc48

119 – The historic steam train that travels along the Douro Line between Régua and Tua from June to October.

FRANCE

ANDUZE TO SAINT-JEAN-DU-GARD

Departure: Anduze
Arrival: Saint-Jean-du-Gard
Distance: 13.5 km (8.4 miles)
Duration: 40 minutes (nonstop)
Stages: 2
Country: France

120/121 – The colorful Cévennes steam train travels along a viaduct.

121 – The steam locomotive maneuvers to connect with the front of the train at the Saint-Jean-du-Gard station.

The Cévennes Steam Train

A small railroad with a steam train in the South of France, where one can also experience the thrill of traveling in the cab alongside the driver.

The **Cévennes steam train** is a tourist service that travels in the Cévennes area of the South of France between the stations of Anduze and Saint-Jean-du-Gard in the summer. The Cévennes mountains range along the southeastern edge of the Massif Central, protected by UNESCO as a Mediterranean agro-pastoral cultural landscape. The train runs along what remains of the Lézan – Saint-Jean-du-Gard railroad, inaugurated on May 26, 1909. It was used for passenger and freight traffic, especially for the Gardon Valley's silk industry. Passenger traffic ceased in 1940 due to the war. In the 1950s, the line was used for freight, especially to move lumber produced in the local woods, but over the years, traffic progressively decreased, and France's national railways decided to permanently close the line on July 31, 1971.

The short railway seemed doomed to have its tracks and infrastructure dismantled. Fortunately, the association CITEV (Compagnie internationale des trains express à vapeur) managed to turn the 13.5 kilometers (8.4 miles) of track between Anduze and Saint-Jean-du-Gard, the most scenic part of the line with numerous bridges and tunnels, into a tourist railroad. The project, which was no easy task, became a reality on June 3, 1982. It has been a great success, carrying over 30,000 tourists each summer. In 1986, management of the tourist line was taken over by the "Train à vapeur des Cévennes" association, which was turned into a company the following year.

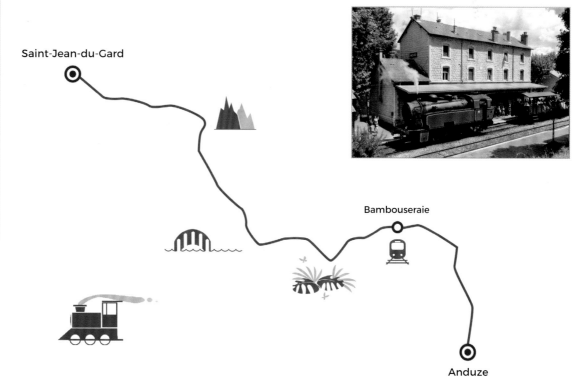

Saint-Jean-du-Gard

Bambouseraie

Anduze

The railway may be short, but the route is extremely scenic, with a great deal of variety.

As soon as the train leaves Anduze, the track enters a tunnel 883 meters (about half a mile) long and upon exiting takes a large metal bridge 104 meters (341 feet) in length over the Gardon river. Here, the route passes between the two rocky massifs of Saint Julien and Peyremale, whose location earned them the nickname of the "Door of the Cévennes." The railway travels through two other valleys with beautiful stone viaducts until it reaches the Bambouseraie station.

This station was specifically built for the tourist railway so passengers could visit the Bambouseraie Botanical Garden, a private garden that is considered one of the most beautiful in France. Covering about 12 hectares (30 acres), its main feature is a collection of over 1,000 species of bamboo, including giant bamboo over 20 meters (65 feet) tall. The park, founded in 1855 by the botanist Eugéne Mazel, is not exclusively dedicated to these plants, however: there are also rhododendrons, maples, azaleas, water lilies, lotuses, palms, and a colossal ginko biloba more than 30 meters (nearly 100 feet) high.

Leaving the Bambouseraie, the line enters the most meandering section of the route. It traverses the 114-meter-long (374-foot-long) Tunnel de Prafrance then takes the large eleven-arch viaduct crossing the confluence of the Gardon de Mialet and the Gardon de Saint-Jean-du-Gard. It is certainly one of the most beautiful points on the line, with stops afterward at Corbès and Torais-Lasalle stations. Stations that were so close together, within a few miles, were the norm along secondary lines like this one, created specifically to serve the small towns in the territories traveled. In this section, one of the most significant engineering works is the **curved bridge** with seven arches standing over the Gardon river. Here, the line approaches the Saint-Jean-du-Gard station but first takes another six-arched masonry bridge on the way to Lasalle and its last tunnel 157 meters (515 feet) in length.

The steam locomotives at the head of the long trains, also composed of open carriages that allow you to easily admire the landscape, have been the subject of long and complex restorations. Three tank locomotives are currently in service, coming from various origins and built between 1937 and 1953. In addition to these vehicles, there is also a historic diesel-powered railcar, built by Renault in 1937. In the high season, there are four daily departures from Anduze station and four in the opposite direction from Saint-Jean-du-Gard. The journey takes about forty minutes, and travelers can choose between return or one-way tickets.

PRACTICAL TIPS

THE STEAM TRAIN TRAVELS THROUGHOUT THE YEAR: DAILY FROM JULY TO OCTOBER, AND TUESDAYS, WEDNESDAYS, AND SUNDAYS IN THE OTHER MONTHS.

USEFUL WEBSITES
Train à Vapeur des Cévennes:
https://www.trainavapeur.com

Bambouseraie en Cévennes botanical garden:
https://www.bambouseraie.fr/en/homepage

INTERESTING FACTS

Who wouldn't like to **travel in the cab** of a steam locomotive, and perhaps make an attempt at shoveling coal into the firebox, watching the driver at the controls? On the Cévennes steam train, this unforgettable experience is available if booked in time. The package includes taking part in creating steam pressure in the locomotive as early as 7:30 in the morning and then getting into the cab with the driver and the stoker, accompanying them on two complete round trips. The two experienced engine operators will offer explanations of how the locomotive works, the controls in the cab, and how connecting rods are lubricated, and water will frequently be supplied to the boiler. It is an opportunity to understand what this fascinating and very tiring job was like in the last century, one not to be missed.

122 – The spectacular 104-meter-long (about 340-foot-long) metal bridge over the Gardon river near Anduze, behind it one of the two rocky spurs called the "Door of the Cévennes."

123 – The steam locomotive maneuvers to connect with the front of the train at the Saint-Jean-du-Gard station.

Corsica Railways

From Calvi to Ajaccio: discovering the island's innermost hidden areas, between the green Vizzavona Forest and the Mediterranean blue.

Corsica is a beautiful island with a very strong identity that a journey by train can reveal, slowly. The meter-gauge **Corsican railway network** connects the two departmental centers of Ajaccio (Corse-du-Sud) and Bastia (Haute-Corse), with a branch from the intermediate Ponte Leccia station to the Balagne coast and to the communes of L'Île-Rousse and Calvi. It performs a regular public transportation service, but due to the features of the route and areas it travels, the train is also of value to tourists. In the Corsican language, the railway is nicknamed *u trinichellu* ("little train"), or alternatively **"the boneshaker,"** a reference to the continual shaking endured while traveling in the old railcars. The service is managed today by the regional company Chemins de fer de la Corse (CFC), which operates completely autonomously from the French state-owned railway, the SNCF.

The south-to-north Bastia – Ajaccio route is 158 kilometers (about 98 miles) long, while the Ponte Leccia – Calvi branch extends for 74 kilometers (46 miles). The service is performed using diesel railcars of various classes, twenty-three of them in all. Twelve of them are CFD AMG 800 railcars and the most modern, having entered into service beginning in 2007. The towed vehicles are former railcars of various types, which have been depowered and refurbished for the purpose.

The railroad line travels alongside roads only for short stretches, and the train thus becomes an excellent means of discovering areas of Corsica, especially its most inland areas, which by car would be almost unreachable.

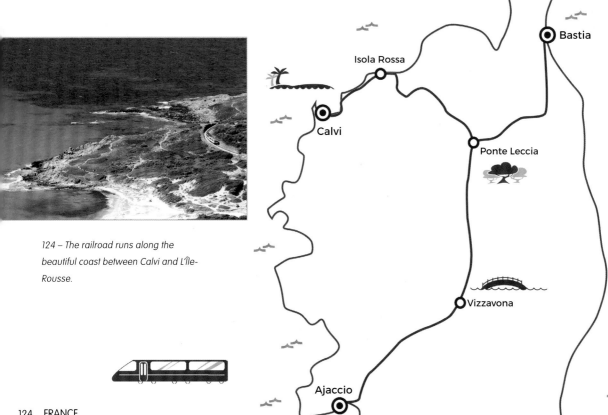

124 – The railroad runs along the beautiful coast between Calvi and L'Île-Rousse.

Departure: Calvi
Arrival: Ajaccio
Distance: 186 km (115 miles)
Duration: 5 hours
Stages: 1 (with optional intermediate stops)
Country: France

124/125 – The route of the railroad between Ajaccio and Bastia meanders a great deal, crossing numerous viaducts and bridges.

PRACTICAL TIPS

ALL INFORMATION NEEDED FOR HASSLE-FREE TRAVEL CAN BE FOUND ON THE CORSICAN RAILWAYS' WEBSITE, WHICH IS SIMPLE BUT COMPREHENSIVE. THERE IS A WIDER AVAILABILITY OF TRANSPORTATION NEAR THE CITIES OF AJACCIO, BASTIA, AND CALVI, WHICH HAVE SUBURBAN SERVICES TO THE TOWNS OF MEZZANA, CASAMOZZA, AND L'ÎLE-ROUSSE RESPECTIVELY. A SEPARATE TIMETABLE ILLUSTRATES THE CONNECTIONS BETWEEN THE THREE CITIES: BASTIA – AJACCIO – BASTIA, AJACCIO – CALVI – AJACCIO, AND BASTIA – CALVI– BASTIA.

INTERRAIL TICKETS AND OTHER CONCESSIONS PROVIDED BY THE FRENCH RAILWAYS ARE NOT ACCEPTED, BUT THERE ARE DISCOUNT CARDS, WHICH ONE CAN USE TO TRAVEL FREELY THROUGHOUT THE NETWORK FOR SEVERAL DAYS AT A REDUCED PRICE.

USEFUL WEBSITES
https://www.balagne-corsica.com

https://www.musee-maisonbonaparte.fr

https://www.musee-fesch.com

https://cf-corse.corsica

It can also snow heavily in the mountains in winter, and the train, fitted with a snowplow, is the only vehicle that guarantees a connection between many inland cities during challenging times.

The stations have maintained the charm of bygone days iinside and outside, as evidenced by the ticket office at the Francardo station. Both lines aslo offer beautiful views, but for those desiring a combination of both sea and mountains within a single trip, the route from Calvi to Ajaccio (or vice versa) is not to be missed. The stretch from Calvi to L'Île-Rousse winds along the coast, offering scenic views of bays and beaches that are often **unreachable by car**. This stretch, with its intermediate stops, has actually been renamed the *tramway de la Balagne*. It is very popular with swimmers due to its sixteen intermediate stops, providing a real service to the beaches.

The route then begins to climb toward Ponte Leccia through woods and valleys that can only be reached via hiking trails. At this station, the track merges with the line coming from Bastia and continues south toward Corte and Vizzavona, crossing Corsica's Regional Natural Park.

126 – The Île della Pietra, in the municipality of L'Île-Rousse, is uninhabited. Atop it stands a lighthouse and the ruins of an old coastal watchtower.

127 top – The Église Saint-Jean-Baptiste overlooks the small port of Bastia.

127 center – The dazzling Bay of Calvi. It is dominated by the citadel built by the Genoese in the thirteenth century containing a network of sloped cobblestone streets.

127 bottom – The train makes many stops serving the beaches between Calvi and L'Île Rousse.

This is one of the most spectacular stretches of the route due to its numerous suspended bridges dozens of feet above the valley floor. Among them, the bridge designed by the engineer **Gustave Eiffel** is particularly famous. In the commune of Vivario, with the structure supporting the track at an 84-meter (about a 275-foot) height, Eiffel's bridge is constructed of metal lattice beams atop stone piers. Between the curves, tunnels, and bridges in this area, the line overcomes a 450-meter (about 1,500-foot) height difference within just 17 kilometers, or about 10.5 miles, of track.

Having reached Vizzavona, whose station with its 906-meter (almost 3,000-foot) height is the highest in Corsica and a well-known starting place for hikers from all over Europe, the train slips into the Vizzavona Tunnel, 3,916 meters (2½ miles) long, flowing into the Gravona Valley. The journey continues amid a typical mountain landscape among dense, coniferous woods. On the

128 top – On the Ajaccio – Bastia line, the famous metal bridge designed by Gustave Eiffel crosses the Vecchio river near Vivario.

descent toward Ajaccio, the conifers are progressively replaced by chestnut trees and then, further down, by vegetation typifying the Mediterranean coast.

Ajaccio, Bastia, Calvi, and the many locations between are worth visiting in order to explore their interesting features. In Calvi's old town, the indoor market is especially fascinating; there one can find the island's finest culinary specialties. In the island's second city of Bastia, the historic center and its numerous civic and religious monuments cannot be missed. In Napoleon's birthplace of Ajaccio, in addition to locations linked to the great general such as the Maison Bonaparte and to the cathedral, the Palais Fesch is also highly interesting. The museum houses one of the most impressive collections of Italian art from the fourteenth to the eighteenth century, its prominence deemed second only to the Louvre in France.

INTERESTING FACTS

One of the most enchanting places in Corsica is Vizzavona, which is easily accessed via the Ajaccio – Bastia railway. Here the great forest of Vizzavona extends for 1,500 hectares (3,700 acres) along the slopes of the Col de Palmente and Monte d'Oro. The setting is fantastic for mountain and hiking enthusiasts: at elevations between 800 and 1,650 meters (2,625 and 5,413 feet), the slopes are blanketed in a dense forest of great beeches and larch pines, the latter a subspecies of *Pinus nigra* found only in Corsica, Calabria, and Sicily. The commune of Vizzavona only developed following the construction of the railroad in the late nineteenth century, when the area's pleasant climate and the beauty of the landscape made it an early tourist resort for the wealthy landowners of Ajaccio. The station still sits at the town's center today, with beautiful houses from the last century scattered among the surrounding woods.

128 bottom – The small Vivario station in the heart of Corsica, between Ajaccio and Bastia.

129 – The track near Vivario is very challenging, with bridges, viaducts, and sections carved into rock.

ITALY
CATANIA TO RIPOSTO

Departure: Catania
Arrival: Riposto
Distance: 110 km (68 miles)
Duration: About 3 hours and 15 minutes
Stages: 2
Country: Italy

130/131 – A pair of Circumetnea
railcars pass an old lava flow on the
slopes of Mount Etna in Sicily.

Circumetnea Railway

A journey to the authentic Sicily on the slopes of Etna: from Catania to Riposto, traveling between lava flows, citrus groves, and prickly pears.

Mount Etna is the highest, most prominent volcano in Europe, overlooking eastern Sicily and the city of Catania from a height of 3,357 meters (11,014 feet). Thanks to the **Circumetnea Railway**, discovering this volcano by train is an opportunity easily within anyone's reach.

This narrow-gauge railroad, built between 1895 and 1898, starts from the city of Catania by the sea. With an almost **circular route** of about 110 kilometers (68 miles), it stops at all major residential centers on the west, north, and northeast sides of the volcano. Etna's slopes are intensely cultivated, up to about a 1,000-meter (3,280-foot) elevation, and the train takes passengers through citrus and olive groves, as well as dense prickly pear plantations. The highest part of the volcano, meanwhile, is characterized by spontaneous vegetation alternating with expanses of now-petrified lava, a sign of past eruptions. The top of the volcano is often already whitened with snow by autumn. The landscape is unique, and UNESCO listed Mount Etna as a World Heritage Site in 2013.

The rail line, which allows passengers to easily visit these spectacular places, departs from Catania Borgo station on Via Caronda, in front of which sits an old FCE no. 14 steam locomotive, one of the line's first in service. The railroad is single-track, with a narrow 950-millimeter gauge (just over 3 feet wide), and is not electrified. The service is carried out by contemporary Newag "Vulcano" diesel railcars, as well as some ADE railcars, which, while more dated, might be in better harmony with the landscape traveled.

131 – Mount Etna, about 3,357 meters (about 11,000 feet) high, dominates the eastern part of Sicily. The Circumetnea line travels along its slopes on a circular path.

PRACTICAL TIPS

FOR A CIRCULAR ROUTE WITH A DEPARTURE AND ARRIVAL IN CATANIA, GET OFF AT GIARRE STATION INSTEAD OF RIPOSTO, THEN TAKE A NATIONAL RAIL TRAIN ON THE MESSINA – CATANIA LINE.

USEFUL WEBSITES
Circumetnea Railway, with up-to-date information:
https://www.circumetnea.it

Catania Metropolitan Transport Company (AMT) :
https://catania.mobilita.org

132 – A spectacular overview of the city of Catania, with the port in the foreground and Mount Etna, with a plume of smoke, in the background.

133 top left – Randazzo is one of the most beautiful places along Etna's slopes that is reachable by train.

The line performs a daily service connecting the city of Catania to towns on the slopes of the volcano. One important feature for those wishing to explore Etna by train is that the Circumetnea Railway allows travelers to bring their bicycles on board at no additional cost, as opposed to the ticket required on many trains. This allows passengers to alight at an intermediate station for a two-wheel excursion before continuing or returning by train. Along the way are also numerous simple stops in the open countryside. These **stops are optional** and until recently were used frequently by farmers to reach their plots of land for cultivation. Today, if one asks the train staff to make one of these stops, they also provide an excellent starting point for excursions on the slopes of the volcano.

Departing from Catania Borgo, the train heads toward the outskirts of the city, skirting the houses and crossing traces of the lava flow that had reached, and destroyed, Catania in 1669.

The first stop is Misterbianco, after which, to the right in the direction of the mountain, passengers can see the spectacular landscape of densely cultivated countryside from their windows. The maximum speed on this very circuitous line is 60 kilometers

Travelers can construct their own itineraries by consulting the railway's website, where they can find updated timetables and details about its bicycle transport service, as well as some tour suggestions. Those who would like to combine the train trip with a bicycle excursion can rent a bike at the AMT (the Metropolitan Transport Company; the cost is covered in the Circumetnea ticket price) or at the many facilities that offer bike hire specific tours. The train ride from Catania to Randazzo takes about two hours, and from Randazzo to Riposto an hour and ten minutes. One can, of course, walk the entire line or, once you arrive at Randazzo, visit the town for a few hours then return on a Randazzo – Catania train.

(37 miles) per hour, perfect for peacefully enjoying the view. On this side are Paternò, Biancavilla, and Adrano stations, exemplifying the local architecture. The track ascends, already reaching a height of 500 meters (1,640 feet), and the landscape becomes increasingly harsh. The train passes by lava flows dating back to various eras until, following Bronte station, it cuts across a spectacular flow of ropy lava.

The train heads to the Maletto plateau, which at 1,000 meters (3,280 feet) is the highest point of the route, and from which visitors can easily admire the **top of the volcano**. The line then reaches Randazzo, the most prominent town the Circumetnea serves. Here, passengers can stop to visit the historic center. The journey continues with a descent along the Alcantara Valley, famous for its spectacular gorges, which themselves merit a special excursion, stopping at Linguaglossa, Piedimonte Etneo, Giarre, and Riposto stations, where the journey ends. Those who would like to return to Catania more quickly, still via rail, can get off at Giarre, where they can board one of the ordinary state railway trains on the Messina – Catania line.

The Circumetnea is thus an excellent way to visit Etna and its slopes. After all, whether it is beautiful Catania with its famed Elephant Fountain and cathedral, its unmissable rice arancini and brioche with granita, or Randazzo with its three basilicas, Sciarone Park, and Lake Gurrida, any location on the train's route allows for impressive experiences and discoveries.

133 bottom left – Excursions on Mount Etna also take visitors to the famous Valle del Bove ("Valley of the Ox"), the epicenter of a recent major eruption.

133 right – Two Circumetnea railcars meet at Randazzo. This location is also an excellent starting point for hikes on the volcano.

Trenino Verde

Small narrow-gauge trains that carry passengers to the most beautiful, hidden, and unspoiled areas of Sardinia.

To mention Sardinia is to conjure thoughts of beautiful beaches, dreamlike coves, and crystal-clear water. But there is another, equally beautiful but little-known Sardinia that can be discovered traveling on the vintage cars of the **Trenino Verde** ("Little Green Train"), along the narrow-gauge tracks of the secondary lines running from the coast to its wildest, most unspoiled interior.

Built between the end of the nineteenth century and the first decades of the twentieth, to pull the island's interior from age-old isolation the Sardinian **secondary railway network** has a fascinating and complicated history.

Then, as they are today, roads were scarce and rough. But with the advent of mass auto use that began in the 1970s, the line experienced a progressive decline. Fortunately, not all lines have been closed or dismantled. From the 1990s, thanks to the development of "slow" tourism and the beauty of the line's surroundings, a restoration project was developed, financed by the EU and sponsored by nonprofits WWF Italia and Italia Nostra, saving certain lines and part of the historic rolling stock.

134 – The Trenino Verde, towed by a marvelous FDS 400 locomotive built in 1931, climbs along the slope toward Villanova Tulo on the line to Arbatax.

1	**Departure:** Palau
	Arrival: Tempio Pausania
	Distance: 59 km (36 miles)
	Duration: 3 hours and 30 minutes
	Stages: 1
	Country: Italy
2	**Departure:** Macomer
	Arrival: Bosa
	Distance: 46 km (28 miles)
	Duration: 2 hours and 15 minutes
	Stages: 1
	Country: Italy
3	**Departure:** Mandas
	Arrival: Laconi
	Distance: 37 km (23 miles)
	Duration: 2 hours and 45 minutes
	Stages: 1
	Country: Italy
4	**Departure:** Mandas
	Arrival: Seui
	Distance: 72 km (45 miles)
	Duration: 4 hours
	Stages: 1
	Country: Italy
5	**Departure:** Arbatax
	Arrival: Gairo
	Distance: 62 km (38 miles)
	Duration: 4 hours
	Stages: 1
	Country: Italy

Today they are managed by the regional company ARST (Azienda Regionale Sarda Trasporti), which deals with regional public transportation on the island.

The Trenino Verde lets passengers take a step back in time and experience the train-travel experience of a century past as the train makes its way from the coast, exploring a territory where little has changed. The railway preserves toll booths and stations as they were, as the route winds through a still-wild landscape.

The experience was described by the British writer D. H. Lawrence, famous for the novel *Lady Chatterley's Lover.* A century ago, in the first days of January 1921, Lawrence traveled Sardinia with his wife, Frieda, from south to north on Sardinia's small secondary railway trains, which then were all steam-powered. The couple, both true globe-trotters ahead of their time, were so impressed by the trip that Lawrence wrote a book entitled *Sea and Sardinia,* which contains the following passage: "It is a queer railway. I would like to know who made it. It pelts up hill and down dale and round sudden bends in the most unconcerned fashion."

The word "pelts" sounds a bit strange, because the average speed of the **Little Green Train** is 20 kilometers—less than 12.5 miles—per hour, unthinkable for a public transportation service, but ideal for discovering the interior of Sardinia.

To travel as it was done a century ago is fascinating, but it requires a slightly adaptive spirit. The vintage cars have no electrical sockets or padded seats, there is no bar on board, and it is not possible to bring a bicycle along.

The Trenino Verde runs throughout the year, but there is more availability in summer. Ticket prices are low, and ARST buses can also be used to reach departure stations. Steam trains unfortunately do not run in summertime, following fire prevention regulations established by the Region of Sardinia.

There are three kinds of Trenino Verde trips: "relaxing" trips, short and easy rides suitable for everyone, including the elderly and children; longer "excursions" of about two hours excluding stops, for which it is advisable to bring snacks and a water bottle; and "challenging" trips, rather long journeys of up to three and a half hours, not including stops, in the most uncontaminated and remote areas of the island. On such trips, it is useful to wear clothing appropriate for hiking.

Even those who are not train and locomotive enthusiasts will be fascinated by the **historic vehicles** employed on the Trenino Verde: ADe diesel-powered railcars, built in the early 1950s by the Officine Meccaniche della Stanga, which are 17 meters (about 56 feet) long and

can travel along curves with a radius of less than 100 meters (328 feet) **(half the minimum radius of ordinary railways)** and carry up to 55 people. Then there are 72-seat V2D passenger cars, built in the 1930s, pulled by a small LDe diesel locomotive. The shining gem of the line, however, is a group of **steam locomotives**: an FCS 5 built by Breda in 1914, an SFS 5, also by Breda, from 1930, and an FCS 400 built by the Officine Meccaniche Reggiane in 1931, as well as some magnificent wooden Bauchiero carriages from 1913. These technical jewels have been allowed back into operation thanks to a careful restoration process.

There are five itineraries the Trenino Verde offers, which run throughout the island:

1. PALAU – TEMPIO

The 59-kilometer (10.5-mile) Palau – Tempio Pausania trip takes place along the Sassari – Palau line in the island's north. It lasts about three and a half hours, and the train departs from the Palau city stop, a few hundred yards from the Palau Marina terminal station. The route travels across the whole of Gallura and leads from the sea to Tempio, the highest point of the entire line at about 550 meters (over 1,800 feet) above sea level. The landscape is characterized by cork oaks and granite. Stops for excursions and visits of varying lengths are planned

PRACTICAL TIPS

RIDES ON THE LITTLE GREEN TRAIN INCLUDE BOTH OUTBOUND AND RETURN JOURNEYS, BUT IT IS POSSIBLE TO BREAK UP OR SHORTEN THE EXCURSION BY RETURNING (OR HEADING OUT) ON AN ARST BUS, OR SLEEPING IN A B&B OR HOTEL ALONG THE WAY. THE TRENINO VERDE TRAVELS THROUGHOUT THE YEAR AND HAS A CALENDAR PROVIDED ON ITS WEBSITE. THE TICKET HAS A SINGLE RATE FOR THE ENTIRE LINE AND PROVIDES PASSENGERS WITH THE RIGHT TO GET ON AND OFF AT ANY STATION ON THE SCHEDULE. WHEN PURCHASING TICKETS ON THE PLATFORM, TRAVELERS MUST CHECK TRAIN AND SEAT AVAILABILITY FOR THE CHOSEN DAY.

USEFUL WEBSITES:
http://www.treninoverde.com

In addition to offering travel on historic trains, the Trenino Verde also has a museum, located in the Monserrato station. In a space of about 1,000 square meters (about a third of a square mile), it houses numerous artifacts relating to the history of secondary railways in Sardinia. The museum is divided into different areas: The first is dedicated to material connected to the construction phase of narrow-gauge railway lines in Sardinia. A second illustrates the work, tools, and machinery used in the workshops, while another concerns the operation of the old stations, with equipment utilized by the station masters, in addition to timetables and other documentation. A fourth section houses historical rolling stock: in addition to parts from vintage rolling stock and other material, some steam locomotives—a Winterthur No. 43 "Goito" from 1983 and a Reggiane FCS 402 from 1931—are kept here, alongside some historic cars.

to Arzachena, Lake Liscia, and, of course, Tempio Pausania, where travelers can also visit the railroad museum.

2. MACOMER – BOSA

The journey on the Macomer – Bosa line, 46 kilometers (28.5 miles) long, takes an average of two hours and fifteen minutes. Opened for service in 1888, it is one of the first routes built on the island. The first part of the journey is through the Campeda plateau, over 500 meters (over 1,600 feet) high. It then slowly descends towards Tresnuraghes and Bosa on the coast, considered one of the most beautiful villages in Italy for its houses painted in bright pastels.

3. MANDAS – LACONI

The Mandas – Laconi route is a journey of about 37 kilometers (23 miles) that follows the Mandas – Sorgono line (the latter is reached by the Trenino Verde on some special occasions). The trip takes about two hours and forty-five minutes. The route crosses the Barbagia di Belvì, stopping at various towns, and it includes breaks in Isili to view the famous Nuraghe Is Paras, considered one of the most beautiful extant examples of Sardinia's ancient stone structures. The train also stops in Nurallao and in Laconi, where it is interesting to, among other things, explore the Museum of Menhir Statues.

4. MANDAS – SEUI

This trip winds along the Mandas – Arbatax railway line and is 72 kilometers (45 miles) long, lasting approximately four hours. The train travels through the wild mountains of Gennargentu, and, after crossing the Flumendosa river, makes a long, panoramic climb amid the pristine mountains of Barbagia, one of the most beautiful and inaccessible areas of Sardinia.

5. ARBATAX – GAIRO

This route winds along the Arbatax – Mandas railway line and is 62 kilometers (38.5 miles) long. The duration of the trip, including stops, is about four hours. The journey begins at the Arbatax station, amid the fishermen's boats by the Cala dei Genovesi. After stopping at Tortolì, the train heads inland and climbs toward the towns of Elini and Lanusei, with sweeping views of the sea. The journey then continues, stopping at Lake Bau Muggeris (Lago Alto del Flumendosa) then arriving at Gairo Taquisara. Here, passengers can visit the ghost towns of Osini Vecchio and Gairo Vecchio, abandoned in 1951 after a devastating flood.

Travelers can organize their trip completely on their own, but they can also rely on the "Trenino Verde Point," a network of independent local tour operators who can not only arrange the journey by train but also offer additional services including hospitality, excursions with local expert guides, and suggestions for special places to explore.

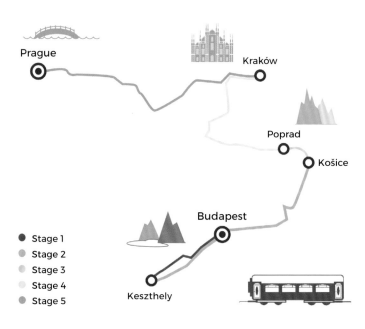

The Golden Eagle Danube Express

An itinerary from Budapest to Prague that combines architectural masterpieces with a fascinating vision of modern European culture and traditions.

The **Golden Eagle Danube Express** is a luxury tourist train that allows passengers to travel between the most enticing cities in Eastern Europe. It is operated by Golden Eagle Luxury Trains, a British tour operator specializing in this kind of service, which also operates similar trains in Russia, Central Asia, and China. The format of all these trips is quite similar: travelers are welcomed aboard the train, which for a week or more serves as their **five-star hotel on wheels**, stopping at various locations organized for the trip. On each of these trips, passengers alight and visit a chosen city or location with guided tours, exactly as one would on a cruise ship.

The train, and the luxury it provides, are certainly a significant part of the experience, but they are not the heart of the journey, which is effectively a sightseeing trip in the vein of a classic tourist package. One could say, with a hint of irony, that, instead of changing hotels at each stop, passengers take their hotel along with them from city to city, and while aboard they can relive the charm of long journeys on the great international express trains of a century ago.

The routes that the train travels each year change, and those wishing to experience a pleasure trip aboard the Golden Eagle Danube Express should spend some time consulting the company's website. One can also contact a specialized tour operator to find out what seasonal tourist packages and itineraries are available.

Prague · Kraków · Poprad · Košice · Budapest · Keszthely

Stage 1
Stage 2
Stage 3
Stage 4
Stage 5

Departure: Budapest
Arrival: Prague
Distance: 1,550 km (963 miles)
Duration: 7 days
Stages: 5
Country: Hungary, Slovakia, Poland, Czech Republic

140 top – A luxurious, welcoming compartment of a Golden Eagle Danube Express coach.

140 bottom – A piano in the spacious lounge car stands ready for staff to entertain passengers on the journey between Budapest and Prague.

140/141 – The train crosses a natural landscape of immense beauty.

PRACTICAL TIPS

USEFUL WEBSITES
https://www.goldeneagleluxurytrains.com

Tatra Mountains Electric Railway:
https://www.vlaky.net/zeleznice/spravy/5557-TEZ-v-premenach-casu

142 – Budapest at sunset, with the outstanding Hungarian Parliament Building on the banks of the Danube.

143 top right – The chapel in the Wieliczka Salt Mine near Kraków. The mind was used for salt extraction from the thirteenth century up until 1996 and is one of the oldest salt mines in the world.

Some routes are periodically repeated, such as the Transylvanian East tour from Budapest to Istanbul, but new routes are also introduced, like the Central European Classics tour, with an itinerary of Budapest– Keszthely – Košice – Poprad – Kraków – Prague. This journey travels across charming landscapes and captivating cities, combining architectural masterpieces from some of Europe's most significant periods to give fascinating insight into modern European culture and traditions.

The train, departing from Budapest, crosses the Hungarian plain and runs along the south shore of Lake Balaton. It then enters Slovakia, with a visit to the city of Košice and an interesting excursion on the **rack railway** of the Tatra Mountains near Poprad. In Poland, the train makes an unforgettable stop to explore Kraków's Gothic and Renaissance architecture, followed by a tour to discover the fascinating Wieliczka salt mines. The trip ends in Prague, arriving at the main railway station, with a long, pleasant visit in the city.

The train consists of numerous coaches, most of which were built in the 1980s and 1990s then refurbished in the early 2000s. The four beautiful 1950s sleeping and couchette cars that formed part of the **Hungarian presidential train** are an exception and are kept to their original design. In addition to the sleeping and couchette cars, the Danube Express includes two dining cars, a bar car, and a lounge car, as well as two service cars for staff and the onboard generator.

There is a choice of two levels of service. The **Superior Deluxe** cabins, only four to each carriage, offer an extremely comfortable daytime setup, a large sofa and two chairs with two large windows, one of which can be opened (excellent for reflectionless

photos). At night, the cabin transforms into a luxurious UK-standard king-size bed. Of course, a cabin like this has an equally luxurious bathroom and all the comforts of a five-star hotel.

Meanwhile, the Deluxe cabins are slightly smaller (there are five per carriage) and provide two sofas that each turn into a single bed at night, two armchairs, and a bathroom with a shower, along with, of course, all the services typical of a luxury train of this standard. These cabins also have two large windows, one of which can be opened.

The restaurant cars are also very lovely, with luxurious tablecloths, porcelain dishes, and a romantic light at each table. There are tables for two, perfect for a romantic dinner, and for four people, for those perhaps wishing to befriend other passengers.

The lounge car, which also features a magnificent piano, is set up with tables and comfortable armchairs and is the spot where most onboard social life takes place.

All that remains is to decide on one's preferred trip and come aboard for a European city or Balkan tour.

The Tatra Rack and Scenic Railway, which is traveled by Central European Classics passengers, contains two interesting Slovak tourist lines. The Štrbské Pleso – Štrba cog, or rack, railroad has a narrow 1-meter (3.3-foot) gauge. It was built in 1896, then rebuilt again on a narrow gauge in 1970. Thanks to the rack-and-pinion system, in less than 5 kilometers (just over 3 miles) of track, with a **grade of 15%**, it overcomes a difference in height of about 450 meters (nearly 1,500 feet). At its terminus in the valley (Štrba station), it connects to the main standard-gauge line between Bratislava and Košice, while at the mountain terminus (Štrbské Pleso station), it connects to the Tatra Electric Railway. The latter, which also has a narrow one-meter gauge but uses normal adhesion, reaches Poprad 29 kilometers (18 miles) away, which is also on the main Bratislava – Košice line. These trains serve an important tourist area, crossing a landscape of great scenic beauty.

143 left – A bird's-eye view of Festetics Palace in Keszthely, Hungary.

143 bottom right – A classic image of the center of Prague, with the iconic Charles Bridge.

Madaraka Express

On the new railroad line between Nairobi and Mombasa, dedicated to freedom and replacing the "Lunatic Express," a symbol of the colonial era.

In 2017, Kenya introduced the Mombasa-Nairobi Standard Gauge Railway (SGR), a new, modern rail link between its capital of Nairobi and the prominent port city of Mombasa. It has been the country's most significant infrastructure project, its development having started with Kenya's independence in 1963. The aim is for it to become the first segment within a modern railway network connecting to neighboring countries. This express train, connecting the two cities each day without intermediate stops, has been baptized the **"Madaraka Express,"** the train of freedom, or "self-governance" in Swahili. The new connection has freed passengers from earlier journeys between Nairobi and Mombasa, which were long, hard, and hazardous. Prior to the opening of the new railway, which is standard-gauge and single-track, there were only two ways to make the journey between the two cities. One was with the **"Lunatic Express,"** the only train that traveled—in no less than twelve hours, delays excluded—along the old, run-down narrow-gauge line, a relic of the colonial era. The other option was to take an uncomfortable, dangerous journey of about ten hours by bus.

On the Madaraka Express, the new railway line's 485 kilometers (about 300 miles) are traveled in just five hours aboard the new, comfortable trains, equipped with air-conditioning as well as bar and restaurant service.

144 – Many sections of the new railroad line have been built on viaducts like this one in the town of Athi River.

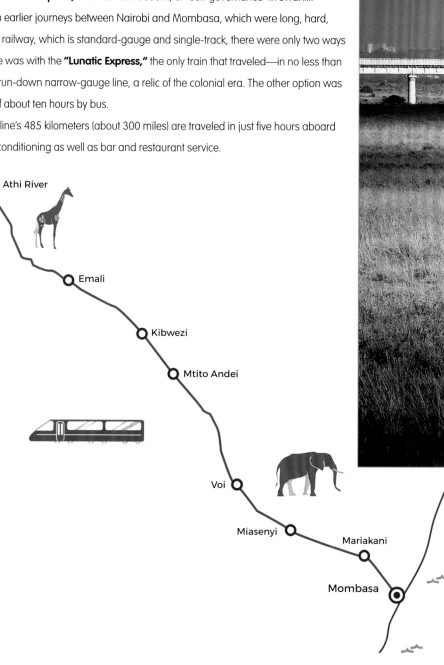

Departure: Nairobi
Arrival: Mombasa
Distance: 485 km (300 miles)
Duration: 5 hours
Stages: 1
Country: Kenya

144/145 – An appealing image of a black rhino on the savanna of Nairobi National Park, Kenya, with the Nairobi skyline and the Madaraka Express viaduct.

THE SGR'S NAIROBI TERMINUS STATION IS OUTSIDE THE CITY OF NAIROBI. KENYA RAILWAYS HAS ORGANIZED A RAIL LINK (ON THE OLD LINE) BETWEEN NAIROBI CENTRAL STATION, IN THE CITY CENTER, AND NAIROBI TERMINUS. THERE ARE ALSO BUS AND TAXI CONNECTIONS. THE MOMBASA STATION IS ALSO OUTSIDE THE CITY CENTER AND CAN BE REACHED BY BUS OR TAXI.

USEFUL WEBSITES
Madaraka Express:
https://krc.co.ke/madaraka-express-passenger-service

146 – A group of impalas walks near the elevated railroad that allows animals to move beneath the tracks near Nairobi.

The train was immediately a huge success, to the point that a second one, a nonstop night train, was also introduced between the two cities, as well as another stopping at all seven intermediate stations on the line.

Traveling on the Madaraka Express is an excellent way not only to visit Kenya's two main cities but to understand the country's heavy investment in its economic development. The train journey is also an excellent opportunity to get to know Kenyans, who use it daily, in an informal and friendly context.

On this route, which is largely parallel to the old, now-closed narrow-gauge railway and to the Nairobi-Mombasa (A109) Road, the train first travels through Nairobi National Park and then the famed Tsavo National Park, so **elephants, gazelles, and giraffes** can be seen quite easily from its large windows. To minimize the train's impact on the parks' animals, this stretch is largely built on an embankment as opposed to the savanna, and fourteen channels have been built under the tracks so animals can move from one side of the railway to the other. The measure is necessary both for the safety of the animals and that of the train, which, traveling at over 100 kilometers (62 miles) per hour, would risk a great deal in the unfortunate event of hitting an elephant.

The stations on the line, all differing from each other, are themselves notable points of interest for their particular architecture, inspired by local elements and motifs. The Nairobi Terminus station, for example, depicts a pair of trains topped by a bridge, while ocean waves provided inspiration for the other terminus of Mombasa. Some of the intermediate stations are very intriguing, like the white-and-brown-striped station at Miasenyi, inspired by a zebra's stripes,

The history of the state of Kenya begins with its railway. The nation has developed around its narrow-gauge line from Mombasa to Nairobi, and then north to Uganda. Everyone came to know this line as the "Lunatic Express" because its construction then seemed like, and perhaps was, actual lunacy. Its construction constitutes both an epic and tragic page in the history of colonialism in Africa. Tens of thousands of workers lost their lives due to accident or illness, though history has dictated that only twenty-eight of them, said to have been devoured by a pair of especially bold lions, should be individually remembered. Eventually, in 1901, the tracks arrived in Kisumu, on the eastern shore of Lake Victoria. After Uganda and Kenya gained independence, the line suffered a progressive decline up until its closure in 2017, when it was replaced by the Madaraka Express. In the future, the new line should continue until it reaches Uganda.

or at Kibwezi, referencing traditional African architecture, its "leaves" providing passengers with shade from the sun.

The **ultramodern trains** in service on this line can carry up to 960 passengers, each with a single buffet car. First class coaches, featuring bright red seats, are configured with two adjacent seats on each side of a central aisle, while in second class, rendered in blue, there are two seats on one side and three on the other. The buffet car, accessible only to first-class travelers, has a row of elegant tables on either side of the central aisle, each with four seats. Second-class passengers meanwhile have access to a minibar service at their seats, modeled on the service provided on airplanes.

In addition to the express train connecting the two cities from Friday to Sunday, there is a train that departs the Nairobi Terminus in the morning with the small station at Suswa as its destination. From there, visitors can take an interesting excursion on the slopes of the Suswa volcano, deep in Maasai territory. Suswa is certainly the least famous volcano in the heart of the Maasai people's land, but it is probably the most interesting of the Great Rift Valley's three well-known volcanoes.

147 top left – A group of zebras quench their thirst in Tsavo West National Park.

147 top right – An excellent view of a group of giraffes in Tsavo East National Park.

147 bottom right – The ultramodern Mombasa station, the endpoint of the new 485-kilometer (300-mile) railroad connecting it to the capital of Nairobi.

Mukaba Express

A trip on the Mukuba Express between Tanzania and Zambia with the locals, on the only train that, in two days' time, travels the 1,860 kilometers (1,156 miles) between Dar es Salaam and Kapiri Mposhi.

Once a week, the **Mukuba Express** connects Tanzania's largest city, Dar es Salaam on the coast of the Indian Ocean, to Kapiri Mposhi (a town just north of Lusaka) near the Copperbelt of central Zambia. The journey is 1,860 kilometers (1,156 miles), with the train running along the Tazara Railway track. To travel on this line is an adventure, one that allows passengers to immerse themselves in the daily life of these two great countries in southern Africa while traversing some of the region's most beautiful areas.

TAZARA is an acronym that stands for the **Tanzania Zambia Railway Authority**, a body that operates the railway and is owned by both states. Opened in 1975, the line is the child of South Africa's apartheid period. Its construction was intended to remove landlocked Zambia from its economic dependence on South Africa and Rhodesia and was executed with economic and technical assistance from China. All manner of difficulties were overcome. For example a team of surveyors had to be employed for over nine months to find a route through **still-unexplored areas**; this now makes up the most rugged section of the route, crossing Tanzania's Udzungwa Mountains. When the line opened to traffic in 1975, the event was hailed as a momentous one for both countries.

Today, the line is traveled by some freight trains and by just two passenger trains covering the entire route. The most important passenger train is the Mukuba Express, which departs every Friday afternoon from Dar es Salaam for Kapiri Mposhi, and in the opposite direction leaves every Tuesday afternoon. The name of the Mukuba Express

148 – *Giraffes in Mikumi National Park; many of the region's wild animals can be admired from the train.*

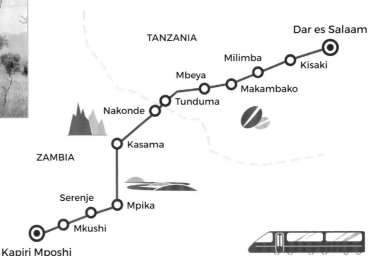

Departure: Dar es Salaam
Arrival: Kapiri Mposhi
Distance: 1,860 km (1,156 miles)
Duration: 46 hours
Stages: 1
Country: Tanzania, Zambia

148/149 – Tazara Railway's Mukuba Express as it navigates the hills of Tanzania's Mbeya region.

is a reference to the mining industry in the "Copperbelt." The metal is Zambia's primary mining export, and the country remains one of its chief producers worldwide.

Apart from the express train, there are two additional trains that stop at all train stops and stations, both in Tanzania and in Zambia. These are also scheduled Tuesdays and Fridays, heading in the opposite direction of the Mukuba Express. When the Mukuba departs Dar es Salaam, the "local" train leaves from Kapiri Mposhi, and vice versa.

The journey between Dar es Salaam and Kapiri Mposhi takes about forty-six hours, but the train very often accrues **significant delays**.

Despite the length of the journey, it is not easy for passengers to become bored since they are able to observe a great variety of wild animals along the way. The process of traversing the most mountainous part of the route is also exciting, traveling through tunnels and past rivers and gorges, thanks to the great deal of engineering work carried out by its contractors.

Of course, daily life in stations and on the train is also a spectacle in its own right. The railroad is very popular with local populations because, despite being slower than a bus trip between the two cities, it is much safer and more affordable. The Tazara railway is a single track with a narrow 1,067-millimeter (42-inch) gauge. From sea level at Dar es Salaam the railway climbs to an elevation of 550 meters (1,804 feet) at Mlimba, then reaches its highest point at 1,789 meters (5,870 feet) between Uyole and Mbeya. It then descends to 1,660 meters (5,446 feet) at Mwenzo, the highest point in Zambia, settling at 1,274 meters (4,180 feet) at Kapiri Mposhi.

Departing from the coast, the line heads west, crossing the Pwani Region. It then heads south of Mikumi National Park, entering the wilderness in the northern part of the Selous Game Reserve, located in the Morogoro Region.

The railway then crosses the Kilombero Valley and runs along the Kibasira Swamp. The next section, 158 kilometers (98 miles) between Mlimba ("the Kingdom of Elephants") and Makambako ("the Place of Bulls"), is the most rugged and demanding, with forty-six bridges and eighteen tunnels. The most spectacular work is the bridge over the River Mpanga, which rests on three piers 50 meters (160 feet) high.

The Mukuba Express then heads to the highlands of Iringa, a coffee and tea region, due to its significantly cooler climate. As the train approaches Makambako, **Udzungwa Mountains National Park** appears to the north, while the Kipengere Range extends to the south. Makambako is a point of exchange between the railway and the Tanzam ("Tanzania-Zambia") highway.

From Makambako, the railway and the highway follow an almost parallel route toward Mbeya, still traveling along the Kipengere mountain range. From the city of Mbeya, both the railroad and the highway head northwest to Tunduma, where they cross the Zambian border.

The Tazara Railway enters northeastern Zambia in the Nakonde district and heads southwest to Kasama. It then turns southward

and crosses the Zambezi River to reach Mpika. After entering the Central Province, the railway runs parallel to the northern slopes of the Muchinga Mountains, passing through Serenje and Mkushi to the New Kapiri Mposhi station a few miles north of Lusaka.

The Mukuba Express offers four different levels of service on board. There are some first-class carriages and cabins with four seats that convert into berths at night. The cabins contain a small table, a lamp, electrical sockets, and a small fan—there is no air-conditioning! The windows can be opened, however. In second class, the cabins are quite similar but have six seats. For those not wishing to share a cabin with other passengers, one can book a full compartment using the family cabin option. Much less comfortable are the seventy-eight-seat Super Seater lounge cars, offering single seats with adjustable arm- and backrests. Finally, for those who truly wish to travel like most of the locals, there are completely spartan **third-class coaches** with single seats running along the sides of the central corridor. The train also includes a basic dining car and a bar car.

INTERESTING FACTS

Tazara had a strong social and economic impact on rural regions along the line. With Tanzania's economic liberalization in the 1990s, villagers began to use the railroad to trade local products. The railroad also allowed settlers to move into the fertile Kilombero River valley between Mbeya and Kidatu and work to produce cash crops, like rice and vegetables, that could be easily shipped to other communities. The railroad, which travels through very diverse regions, facilitates trade between previously isolated communities and has also encouraged large-scale investments, including a hydroelectric power station in Kidatu and a paper mill in Rufiji. Tazara has also become a major employer, and in forty years of activity, as many as one million people have been employed by the railway.

150/151 – The Mikumi National Park in Tanzania offers numerous safaris for getting to know the region's rich wildlife from up close.

Fianarantsoa – Côte Est Railway

An adventurous train ride in Madagascar alongside the region's residents, connecting Fianarantsoa to Manakara on the Indian Ocean (with a measure of uncertainty).

The journey between the city of Fianarantsoa in the central highlands of Madagascar and Manakara, a port town on the southeastern coast of the island, is a true adventure. The railroad that runs between them, the **Fianarantsoa – Côte Est (FCE) railway**, is 163 kilometers (101 miles) long and provides the only connection that small-town and village populations between the two terminal stations have to procure consumer goods as well as to sell their agricultural products and handmade wares. One could even say that the train itself and the railroad almost form **one long marketplace**—somewhere to meet and exchange goods, and an opportunity for locals to get to know each other.

However, despite its social importance, the railroad's infrastructure and rolling stock are not in good condition. Thus, the journey, which ought to take about eight hours, can easily last twelve or even eighteen, depending on how long the train stops at stations to load and unload goods (which always takes at least half an hour), and on any malfunctions that could affect the tracks or the locomotive. In short, this is no trip for tourists seeking trains with panoramic coaches and bar service, but rather for those looking to immerse themselves in the daily life of the many Malagasy living outside the big cities.

152 – The old railroad station in Manakara, of French colonial construction, a terminus on the line to Fianarantsoa.

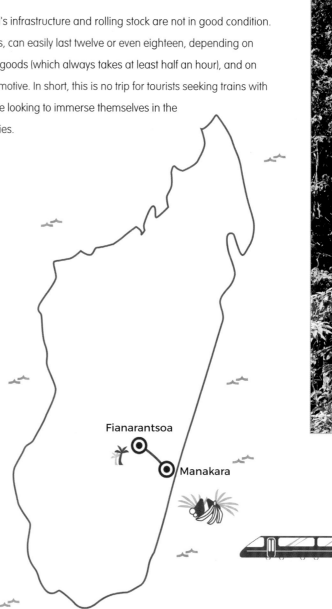

Fianarantsoa

Manakara

Departure: Fianarantsoa
Arrival: Manakara
Distance: 163 km (101 miles)
Duration: 8 hours, approximately
Stages: 1
Country: Madagascar

*152/153 – Traveling on the Fianarantsoa
– Côte Est railroad in Madagascar is
an exciting adventure experiencing the
authentic daily lives of the local people.*

PRACTICAL TIPS

SINCE THE SERVICE IS SO UNPREDICTABLE, IT IS BEST THAT TRAVELERS MAKE A THOROUGH INQUIRY BEFORE EMBARKING ON A TRIP TO MADAGASCAR TO SEE THIS LINE.

USEFUL WEBSITES

The Fianarantsoa – Côte Est (FCE) line's website, which is very basic:
https://www.fce-madagascar.com

Facebook page, which is somewhat more up to date:
https://www.facebook.com/search/top?q=fce-madagascar%20ofisialy

154 – At each train stop, the station becomes a lively, colorful market involving passengers and the people living in the surrounding area.

155 – The train literally slides into the dense tropical vegetation, and the coaches are filled with the scents of the forest.

With a narrow 1-meter (3.3-foot) gauge, the railroad was completed in 1936, in the middle of Madagascar's colonial period under the French. The goal was to promote the region's economic development by offering an outlet to the sea. The Fianarantsoa – Manakara line is isolated from the other three railway lines on the island. It is not electrified, and its route is very uneven, with sixty-seven bridges, four long viaducts, forty-eight tunnels (the longest of which is 1,072 meters, or two-thirds of a mile), and a significant grade that in some places reaches 3.6%. After all, Fianarantsoa, situated on a plateau, has an altitude of over 1,100 meters (nearly 4,000 feet), while Manakara sits on the shore of the Indian Ocean.

Among the line's curiosities, the most surprising is that in Manakara, the **track cuts across the local airport runway** at a diagonal. Apparently, there are only two other such cases in the world—and fortunately, neither the railway nor the airport experience heavy traffic.

The track, and all the railroad's infrastructure, are generally not in good condition, due to poor maintenance over the past few decades, and to damage caused by the frequent tropical cyclones that hit the island, causing the service long interruptions. The rolling stock is no better: until 2020, the line's equipment consisted of two used Alstom AD16B diesel locomotives, the only ones still operational of the six received from the manufacturer. Three used 1500 series locomotives from Renfe (Spain's national passenger railroad company) were then purchased and came into operation at the beginning of 2021, allowing the service to continue.

Now, a glance at its wagons and cars: in all, there are just six passenger cars and twenty-two freight wagons available. The two trains that, according to the timetable, ought to run five times a week between the two cities usually contain a diesel locomotive, one or two freight wagons, and three passenger cars—a set traveling no faster than 30–40 km/h (20–25 mph) due to bad track conditions.

Yet a genuine rarity in the world of trains can also be found in service: the diesel **"Micheline" ZM-516 railcar "Fandrasa."** The car is of French construction, made in 1952, a luxury vehicle at the time, with only nineteen seats and a bar on board. It can be rented for a ride but is limited to the 21 kilometers (13 miles) between the Fianarantsoa station and Sahambavy. A special track has been built there to turn the vehicle around, since it runs in a single direction.

Passengers will not be bored traveling on this train: the local travelers exude vitality, and outside the window, the wonderful landscape of Madagascar flows by. The railroad runs along a valley where there are only trails and paths, with no roads, and it therefore serves as a point of contact for all the area's inhabitants.

Spontaneous markets, common in Africa, arise along its tracks—not just at stations, but also along the route.

The train's arrival is an event and a business opportunity that no one cares to miss. So, as goods purchased in Manakara or Fianarantsoa are unloaded from the wagons and cars, young people load the valley's agricultural products onto them: bags of rice, large baskets of bananas, and fruits of all kinds are bound for big-city markets. Meanwhile, young women and children try to sell food and all kinds of items to travelers: sweets, meatballs, sausages, fried chicken, meat skewers, shrimp, pancakes, sambos, drinks, spices, green peppers, sweet peppers, vanilla, flowers, and handicrafts.

The train is supposed to stop for half an hour, but if needed, the stop could last an hour or two, and there are therefore no other trains on the line. When all have finished their business, the train operators climb into the cab and repeatedly sound the locomotive's horn, signaling that they are about to depart. Passengers and drivers

alike hope that the train does not have a breakdown, and that there are no obstacles on the track, like a fallen log due to rain, or a small landslide. Should this happen, **everyone comes off the train to help free the track** and resume the journey. With old-fashioned African fatalism, passengers reassure each other that "*mora mora,*" little by little, they will finally reach their destination. Along the way, one finds no shortage of **broken-down locomotives** and wagons, abandoned on a secondary track, or the remains of some old accident.

Local passengers are no longer impressed by the landscape, but those who experience this journey for the first time are enchanted by the lush vegetation, banana plants whose leaves brush along the wagons as they travel, and rice fields, as well as the steep cliff faces, a tunnel more than 800 meters (half a mile) long in Ranomena, the great falls that the train passes via a bridge following Andrambovato station, and the long, 137-meter (450-foot) viaduct in Manampatrana.

On this train, visitors can truly mingle with the locals. The authenticity, the landscape, and the good company make this trip a unique one.

SOUTH AFRICA, BOTSWANA, ZIMBABWE, ZAMBIA, TANZANIA

CAPE TOWN TO DAR ES SALAAM

Departure: Cape Town
Arrival: Dar es Salaam
Distance: 5,800 km (3,604 miles)
Duration: 15 days
Stages: 15
Country: South Africa, Botswana, Zimbabwe, Zambia, Tanzania

156 – One of the most beautiful parts of the journey on the Pride of Africa luxury train is visiting Victoria Falls.

157 – The Pride of Africa's vintage coaches have been carefully restored and retain the atmosphere typical of early-1900s train travel.

Pride of Africa

Southern Africa seen from aboard the continent's most famous luxury train, traveling through five countries on a fifteen-day adventure.

The most beautiful and exclusive of African luxury trains is undoubtedly the **Pride of Africa**, offered by the tour operator Rovos Rail, which specializes in train travel.

The train gives passengers an opportunity to discover many different regions in southern Africa with journeys through South Africa, Namibia, Zambia, Zimbabwe, Tanzania, and Angola, which can last from two or three days to two weeks. Speed, of course, is not the aim of this train, which never travels at a speed exceeding 50 km/h (30 mph), both so passengers can relax and enjoy the view and to ensure a more comfortable ride on the railroad tracks, which on this network are not always perfect.

Those who choose Pride of Africa do so for its style and elegance, which are top-notch. Luxury is the parameter by which each feature of the onboard experience is measured. The train features **vintage, classic coaches** with wood-paneled interiors, masterfully restored to preserve their original appearance while adopting the comforts essential to today's travelers. Many of the coaches date back to the peak colonial days of the 1930s, making Rovos Rail one of the world's leading owners of vintage coaches.

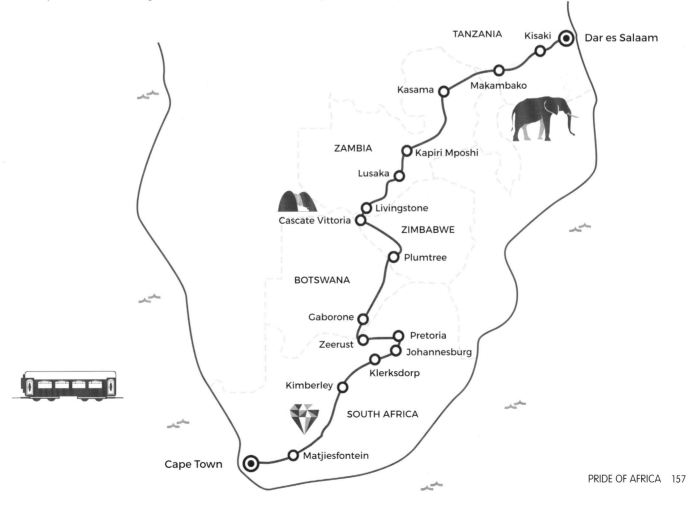

Each of the two Rovos Rail train sets that carry out Pride of Africa tours are able to carry a maximum of seventy-two passengers and contain as many as twenty coaches. There is clearly no lack of space on such a train, whether in the private compartments, which are true hotel suites on a rail, or in the common areas of the train, from the dining cars to the lounge and bar cars, with onboard service guaranteed at the highest level. The twenty coaches masterfully boast the elegance and exclusivity of the **golden age** of long train journeys during the 1920s, mingled with the modern comforts expected by a contemporary seeker of luxury. The trains are air-conditioned, and all thirty-six cabins have private bathrooms. The Royal Suite cabins have an area of 16 square meters (172 square feet), with a private lounge and even a bathroom with bath. Deluxe Suites are "only" 11 meters (118 feet) square but have a private shower and living room, while the more affordable Pullman Suites, which still boast a floor space of 7 square meters (75 square feet), are equipped with a large sofa for daytime that converts into a double bed at night.

158/159 – The sumptuous lounge car at the end of the Pride of Africa train has an open-air space to better observe the fascinating landscape surrounding the train.

158 bottom left – Capital Park station in Pretoria, where the Pride of Africa and all other Rovos Rail tourist trains are based.

158 bottom right – The welcoming interior of the Capital Park station in Pretoria, home of the Pride of Africa.

159 – One of the Pride of Africa's large and luxurious sleeping compartments.

PRACTICAL TIPS

THIS ITINERARY, AND THE OTHERS OFFERED BY ROVOS RAIL, CAN ALSO BE PURCHASED THROUGH MAJOR TOUR OPERATORS. THEY ARE ALSO ABLE TO ORGANIZE ROUND TRIPS WITHIN AFRICA, AS WELL AS ADDITIONAL STAYS IN THE TRAIN'S CITIES OF DEPARTURE AND ARRIVAL.

USEFUL WEBSITES
Rovos Rail: **https://rovos.com**

INTERESTING FACTS

Rovos Rail is the passion project of two South Africans: the founder, Rohan Vos, owner of a spare auto parts business, and his wife, Anthea, both lovers of trains. They took part in an auction of old coaches in 1985, hoping to restore four of them for travel on the South African railways as private family cars. They also bought a 1938 Class 19D steam locomotive, had it restored, and finally, in December 1986, were able to obtain permits to run the train. The exorbitant rate that the railways requested for traffic gave Rohan and Anthea the idea to transform their expensive pastime into a business venture. After more than two years of work, on April 29, 1989, the first Rovos Rail train departed for east Transvaal with four paying passengers, some friends, and some journalists on board.

One very interesting detail underscores both the Pride of Africa's exclusivity and the kind of experience that the train seeks to recreate: there are no radios, televisions, or WiFi on board, and guests are invited to only use mobile phones, laptops, and other twenty-first-century technology in their private cabins. No WhatsApp or Twitter as one dines in the exquisite restaurant cars amid luxury tablecloths, porcelain, and crystal flutes, enjoying dishes prepared by renowned chefs. In this same spirit, passengers are also required to follow the appropriate dress code: on excursions, passengers may wear sportswear, or even hiking gear for those spending time in nature, while at dinner, men are asked to wear a jacket and tie, and women cocktail or evening dresses.

Of course, much of this journey's charm comes from the beautiful sights in the surrounding landscape as well as the places along the railroad, starting with the renowned Victoria Falls, above which the railway passes on a spectacular **steel arch bridge**. South Africa offers extremely diverse environments, from the Karoo desert to the highlands and alpine-like mountains in Lesotho. No less varied and fascinating are its wildlife and other animals, which can be easily seen from the train: among them are plenty of ostriches, which are bred there intensively.

The Pride of Africa travels according to various itineraries, each of them identified by a specific name, ranging from the classic Cape Town tour, a 1,600-kilometer (nearly 1,000-mile) journey between Pretoria, where Rovos Rail is based, and (of course) the ocean city of Cape Town, to the Victoria Falls tour, which lasts three or four nights, to the more demanding Namibia Safari, which, with a 3,400-kilometer (over 2,100-mile), nine-night itinerary, leads up to the coast of the Atlantic Ocean at Walvis Bay. However, one of the most exciting (and expensive) trips that can be made with the Pride of Africa is certainly

the Dar es Salaam, an incredible fifteen-day tour that departs from Cape Town, South Africa, and arrives at the port of Dar es Salaam in Tanzania, on the Indian Ocean.

This epic train journey travels through South Africa, Botswana, Zimbabwe, Zambia, and Tanzania and is one of the most famous in the world. The journey begins in Cape Town and takes guests to the historic village of Matjiesfontein, the diamond-mining city of Kimberley, and the capital of Pretoria for short guided tours, followed by two nights in the Madikwe Game Reserve. It continues through Botswana to Zimbabwe, where guests stay overnight at the Victoria Falls Hotel. After crossing the mighty Zambezi River, the train takes the Tazara Railway in Zambia and continues toward Chishimba Falls, where guests can take a walk on the savanna.

162 top – The panoramic platform at the end of the train also allows passengers to observe the many wild animals in the surrounding natural parks.

162 bottom – The magnificent Chishimba Falls in the Kasama district of northern Zambia.

The train climbs to the border with Tanzania then descends into the **Great Rift Valley**, passing through the spectacular railroad line's tunnels and viaducts. Climbing further, the train crosses the Selous Game Reserve—the largest on the continent, showing an African landscape that can seem frozen in time—before it arrives in Dar es Salaam the next day.

Naturally, the journey can also be made in the opposite direction, starting from Dar es Salaam and arriving in Cape Town.

The gravitational center of these trips is in Pretoria, where the station at Capital Park serves as the Rovos Rail headquarters. Here, in addition to other facilities, the station hosts an ever-expanding **railroad museum**, with the use of old traffic lights and a pedestrian bridge recreating the atmosphere of a rail system of the past. In time, this facility is expected to become one of the most important functioning railroad vehicle museums in the world. Railroad enthusiasts can view the coach and locomotive sheds,

where dedicated teams take care of maintaining rolling stock. The 10,000-square-meter (nearly 12,000-square-foot) workshop spans fifteen tracks, with inspection pits and other special equipment.

The buildings next to the 300-meter (985-foot) platform house laundries, kitchens, and storerooms. This is where all train supply operations take place; they rival those of a world-class hotel in terms of efficiency and attention to detail, all despite the difficulty of having to serve trains traveling thousands of kilometers away.

In the past, many Rovos Rail trains, including the Pride of Africa, were regularly hauled by steam locomotives. This is increasingly difficult today since on the railroad lines being used, especially outside South Africa, there are **fewer and fewer supply points** for the locomotives' water and coal, and fewer turntables to orient them in the right direction. For this reason, steam hauling is limited to certain sections near Pretoria, and the rest of the journey is entrusted to diesel or electric locomotives.

163 top – The train crosses the desert region of the Kalahari in northwestern South Africa.

163 bottom – A glimpse of the Zambezi River, leading to the renowned Victoria Falls on the border between Zambia and Zimbabwe.

RUSSIAN FEDERATION

MOSCOW TO VLADIVOSTOK

Departure: Moscow
Arrival: Vladivostok
Distance: 9,289 km (5,772 miles)
Duration: 7 days
Stages: 1
Country: Russian Federation

164/165 – A passenger train on the Trans-Siberian Railway along Lake Baikal, which the winter has turned to a huge expanse of ice.

The Trans-Siberian Railway

Over 9,000 kilometers (5,500 miles) on the Rossiya express train departing Moscow each day, crossing the continent to reach Vladivostok on the Sea of Japan.

The **Trans-Siberian Railway** is certainly one of the most captivating yet still lesser-known railroad lines in the world. Its history is closely intertwined with Russia's, dating from the time of the czars and lasting into the present day.

It is the longest railroad line in the world, 9,289 kilometers (5,772 miles) long, connecting Russia's capital of Moscow to the city of Vladivostok on the Sea of Japan. The line's construction began in 1891 and ended in June 1904, after meeting all manner of difficulties. Many lives were lost among the tens of thousands of men engaged in the work, who, in addition to freezing winters, overcame mountain ranges, forests, rivers, swamps, and permafrost. From the Ural Mountain city of Chelyabinsk to Vladivostok, the railroad was built in stages until the Circum-Baikal line was completed, resolving the issue of bypassing Lake Baikal. Prior to this section being completed, during summer, both freight and passengers had to cross the giant lake by ship to Mysovaya (now Babushkin), where they could take another train, while in winter, a **temporary railroad was built on the thick ice** on its surface. This colossal feat is calculated to have cost 1,455,000,000 rubles at the end of the nineteenth century, an astronomical figure along the lines of 25 billion dollars today.

165 – The dining car is a place where one can engage in interesting conversations with other passengers, Russian or otherwise, on the long journey.

TRAVELING ON THE TRANS-SIBERIAN RAILWAY IS ABSOLUTELY SAFE. THE HOTTEST PERIOD WITH THE LONGEST DAYS, AND WITH THE MOST TOURISTS, IS FROM MAY TO SEPTEMBER. IN WINTER, THE TRAINS ARE COZY AND HEATED, BUT PASSENGERS MUST DRESS APPROPRIATELY WHEN GETTING OFF. IN IRKUTSK, THE MAXIMUM IS ABOUT -13°C (8.6°F) ON AVERAGE IN JANUARY.

USEFUL WEBSITES
Rossiya tickets:
www.transsiberianexpress.net/train/rossiya

Russian railways website in English: **https://eng.rzd.ru**

The goal of such an effort was to create a trans-Russian railway that would help economically integrate the east, which was uninhabited but rich in natural resources, with the population concentrated in the west. The most important train at the time departed four times a week from St. Petersburg and took twelve days to arrive in Vladivostok. **This train was for a select few**: first class was a truly exclusive experience, in luxurious coaches decorated in mahogany, with bronze finishings and velvet seats. A traveling library, piano, and saloon car completed the first-class experience. However, the price was high: 148 rubles and 15 kopecks, about six months' worth of a worker's wage.

The Russian Revolution and civil war cut off connections to Russia's far east up until 1925, when the service resumed, with just two trains running per month. In September 1966, the **"Rossiya" express train** came into service. It soon became an emblem of the Trans-Siberian Railway, and the most important train to travel along it.

166 left – In Kazan stands the Kul Sharif Mosque, one of the largest mosques in all of Russia.

166 right – An aerial view of the famous Ipatiev Monastery, in what was part of the historic principality of Kostroma.

166/167 – A glimpse of the magnificent Red Square in Moscow, one of the largest squares in the world, along the Kremlin's eastern wall.

167 – An overview of the city of Novosibirsk, Siberia, capital of Novosibirsk Oblast, with the Opera and Ballet Theater in the foreground.

Those who love the railway to the point of traveling on the Trans-Siberian must take a tour of the Moscow Metro to have a look at its most beautiful stations, which are true works of art. In fact, 44 stations out of over 250 are protected as national cultural heritage sites. Visitors will be fascinated by the majesty of the chandeliers and carved frames on their walls, the beauty of their mosaics and painted decoration, the stained-glass windows, their tall columns, and the stateliness of their statues. The most attractive stops are mostly on metro line number 5 (brown), which is the oldest, but others that are no less beautiful can be found on line 2 (dark green) and line 3 (blue). The stations that absolutely cannot be missed include Arbatskaya, which fuses Baroque with traditional elements of Russian architecture, Ploshchad Revolyutsii, with seventy-two life-size bronze statues depicting the people of the Soviet Union, and Slavyansky Bulvar, featuring Art Noveau streetlamps and benches.

168 – A spectacular aerial view of the Trans-Siberian Railway bridge crossing the Irkut river.

Its carriages were red with white Cyrillic lettering, reading "Rossiya" and "Moscow – Vladivostok." Its quality of service was good, with trains departing each day. Central heating, wool comforters, and a kettle with glasses for tea in each cabin kept passengers warm, even while traveling across Siberia in winter. The train also included a children's car and provided political newspapers and books to travelers.

With the fall of the Soviet Union and birth of the Russian Federation, the Rossiya kept running, maintaining its status as the train symbolic of the Trans-Siberian Railway. The only thing that has changed is its livery, and today, its modern coaches bear the red and gray colors of Russian Railways (RZD).

The Rossiya takes passengers on a tour of some of Russia's most interesting cities from west to east, and it can be a stimulating trip. The train connects Yaroslavl, Kazan, Kostroma, Ekaterinburg, Novosibirsk, Irkutsk, Ulan-Ude, Khabarovsk, and (of course) Vladivostok.

Today, there are dozens of tour operators offering rides on the

Trans-Siberian; these are most often carried out on board luxury trains, making the trip feel beutiful but quite unnatural. On the other hand, the trip to Vladivostok on the legendary Rossiya express train, departing Moscow's Yaroslavsky station daily, is a lovely experience and not difficult to organize. The **Rossiya is not a tourist train**. It is used by ordinary passengers to travel between cities along its route of over 9,200-kilometers (5,700 miles) across seven time zones. Yet this is exactly its charm, since it allows passengers to become acquainted with Russia's day-to-day life and immerse themselves in it for nearly a week.

The magnificent landscapes it passes through are also the same that can be admired from the windows of large luxury trains. A ride on the Rossiya lasts 166 hours and 28 minutes, with about **140 stops in cities** along the way, also skirting the fascinating, gigantic Lake Baikal. The train has second- and third-class cars available. Second-class tickets (*kupe* in Russian) provide access to a compartment with four berths (two upper, two lower) and a television, fitted with an access

169 top – A glimpse of the Siberian city of Irkutsk; Circum-Baikal Express tourist trains also depart from Irkutsk station.

169 bottom – A summer view of the Trans-Siberian Railway along Lake Baikal.

control system and a 220V electrical socket. Options are available including or excluding meals.

Third-class cars (*platskart*) have fifty-four beds in an open carriage, divided between upper and lower berths, and are decidedly spartan. The train also has a dining car and a car with hot water and showers for passenger use in both ticket classes.

Reserving and purchasing a ticket is very simple, following a few steps on its website: www.transsiberianexpress.net/train/rossiya (in English). The site also explains bureaucratic information concerning visas and necessary documents.

There are no Russian Railways train tickets that provide for a continuation of one's journey after alighting at an intermediate stop. Passengers deciding to break the trip's seven days into several stages to visit any cities along the train route must therefore purchase tickets for each leg.

It is an exciting experience to travel for so many days

170 top – A dock on the Ussuri river near the city of Khabarovsk, not far from the Trans-Siberian end station in Vladivostok.

aboard the same train, alighting to take a five- to thirty-minute stroll and purchase something at the stations where the Rossiya stops, to meet fellow travelers (very few of whom travel for the full journey), and attempt to speak to them, even without knowing Russian. If you have time, though, it is an excellent idea to make even a one- or two-day stop in some of the cities served by the train.

At least two days could obviously be dedicated to Moscow before departure, perhaps exploring the city using its impressive subway system. The first stop of interest might be Kazan, a major center of Muslim faith in Russia, with its spectacular mosque. Ekaterinburg is a perfect second stop, as it is directly on the border between Europe and Asia. The city boasts a good representation of Russia's symbol of **an eagle with two heads, one facing Europe and one facing Asia**. Irkutsk is another city not to be missed: dubbed the "Paris of Siberia" for its elegant architecture. It is also the gateway to Lake Baikal, with an area the size of The Netherlands, a length of over 600 kilometers (nearly 400 miles) and a depth of over 1,600 meters (over 5,000 feet). Imagine what it looks like completely frozen over in winter. Then

finally comes Vladivostok, serving as not just mere arrival station, but also a symbolic purpose. This begins with the station itself, identical to that of Moscow, which features a complete map of Russia rendered in bas-relief. This station is near the sea, separated from Japan by only 940 kilometers (about 580 miles). A short distance inland, Russia's border with China can be found, not far from its short border with North Korea. One should not wish to stop there for a tourist visit.

170 bottom – The Ivolginsky datsan is a Buddhist complex located near the city of Ulan-Ude in Buryatia, an important hub on the Trans-Siberian Railway.

171 – View of the Zolotoy ("Golden") Bridge, the cable-stayed bridge crossing the Golden Horn Bay in Vladivostok.

The Palace on Wheels

Journeying like the maharajas between the cities and most beautiful places in Rajasthan, the Indian state known for its fortresses and royal palaces.

"Palace on Wheels": there could be no better name for this luxury train, which departs New Delhi station every Wednesday evening for a seven-night, eight-day journey through the most beautiful cities of Rajasthan, a federated state in the north of India, and the country's largest. This region, rich in history, is celebrated for its fortresses and royal palaces, which can still be visited today. It is also known for its natural wonders, including Keoladeo National Park, which has been declared a UNESCO World Heritage Site. The route of the Palace on Wheels also includes a visit to Agra in Uttar Pradesh. The train condenses all the culture and history of this part of India into its sumptuous carriages, bringing passengers to relive the luxurious, somewhat mysterious atmospheres of the different princely states that governed the territory up until the 1940s.

Each of the maharajas had his own magnificent train. The Palace on Wheels draws from this tradition, its carriages named after the Rajput princely states. Fourteen train carriages have therefore been named: Alwar, Bharatpur, Bikaner, Bundi, Dholpur, Dungarpur, Jaisalmer, Jhalawar, Jodhpur, Kishangarh, Kota, Sirohi, and Udaipur.

The Palace on Wheels has an impressive itinerary, traveling through the most beautiful and fascinating places in Rajasthan and Agra. Departing from Delhi, the train passes through: Jaipur, known as the "Pink City" of India; Sawai Madhopur with its wonderful wildlife; Chittorgarh; the romantic district of Udaipur; Jaisalmer and its ancient fortress; Jodhpur; Bharatpur with its bird sanctuary; and Agra, home of course to the Taj Mahal. Such places no

172 – Passengers' welcome aboard the Palace on Wheels is curated to the last detail, starting with its red welcome carpet. Two personal assistants, or khidmutgars, *are available around the clock per coach.*

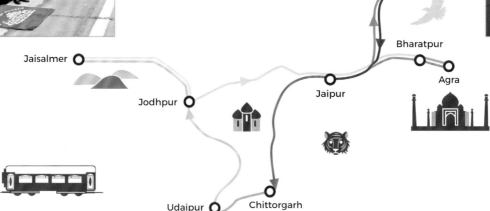

- ● Day 1
- ● Day 2
- ● Day 3
- ● Day 4
- ○ Day 5
- ● Day 6
- ● Day 7
- ● Day 8

New Delhi
Bharatpur
Agra
Jaipur
Jaisalmer
Jodhpur
Udaipur
Chittorgarh

Departure: New Delhi
Arrival: New Delhi
Distance: 2,450 km (1,522 miles)
Duration: 7 nights/8 days
Stages: 8
Country: India – Rajasthan and Uttar Pradesh

172/173 – Jaipur is one place the Palace on Wheels stops. The Amber Fort and Maota Lake are two sites in the city that are worth a visit.

173 bottom – The powerful diesel locomotive, entrusted with the task of pulling the long Palace on Wheels, is fitted with special decorative plaques.

PRACTICAL TIPS

TRAVELERS CAN ADD ONE OR TWO DAYS IN NEW DELHI TO THE TRAIN JOURNEY, BEFORE OR AFTER THE TOUR.
A DRESS CODE IS NOT REQUIRED ABOARD THE TRAIN, BUT IT MUST BE REMEMBERED THAT FOR VISITS TO CERTAIN PLACES, BOTH WOMEN'S AND MEN'S LEGS AND SHOULDERS MUST BE COVERED. COMFORTABLE CLOTHING IS ALSO RECOMMENDED FOR OFF-TRAIN EXCURSIONS, AS WELL AS SOMETHING WARM FOR NATURE PARK VISITS IN THE VERY EARLY MORNING, EVEN IN SPRING AND AUTUMN.

USEFUL WEBSITES
Palace on Wheels:
https://thepalaceonwheels.com

Rajasthan Tourism Development Corporation, Ltd:
https://rtdc.tourism.rajasthan.gov.in

174 top – One of the train's sumptuous lounge coaches, the ideal place for a chat with loved ones or other passengers, or to read a book selected from the train library. The interiors of the more recent coaches were conceived by Indian designer Payal Kapoor and reflect the art of the regions traveled.

174 bottom – The Palace on Wheels offers two dining cars. Pictured is the elegant Maharaja restaurant, serving lavish Indian and international cuisine. The Palace on Wheels' restaurants are especially known for their meals from Rajasthani and Marwari cuisine, and the table settings, from the dishware to the fabrics employed, are just as well prepared.

175 top – Astronomical instruments at the Jantar Mantar observatory in Jaipur. The study of astronomy has very ancient roots in India.

175 center – The fantastic decorations inside the City Palace in Jaipur, a complex of monumental palaces that was once the seat of the maharaja.

175 bottom – The Hawa Mahal (Palace of Winds) in Jaipur was designed by Lal Chand Ustad and shaped to resemble the crown of the Hindu god Krishna.

traveler can ever forget.Established in 1982 to promote Rajasthani tourism and preserve Indian maharajas' antique royal coaches, the Palace on Wheels became **India's first luxury train**. It is practically impossible to find other carriages with similar interiors, which are regal in the literal sense, their designs replicating the lavish halls in the palaces of their time. Beautiful paintings hang on their walls (clad in precious woods), mirrors multiply their spaces, and their furnishings are elegant in their opulence, with fine fabrics and tapestries. Of course, however luxurious these princely coaches may have been, today's necessary comforts, on a train that, in effect, constitutes a five-star hotel, could not have been provided at the time they were constructed.

In the many markets animating the cities of Rajasthan, there is an opportunity to find beautiful handcrafted products. The craft pieces still produced in Rajasthan today are unique and recognized worldwide for their special workmanship and use of color. These objects include jewelry, hand-printed or mirror work fabrics, embroidery work using very fine metal threads, leather items (often of camel leather), ceramics, and many other products. Painted miniatures depicting different stories, for example, have a long tradition and are still renowned today. Rajasthani puppets are also an attraction for tourists. They continue to be widely used by locals, who still give performances, placing them on miniature stages. This authentic form of craftsmanship is still tied to its local traditions and culture.

For this reason, they have been subject to renovations, carried out with respect for their history. This is especially true of the two dining cars, the lounge car, and the bar car, whose interiors have been preserved. The Palace on Wheels is made up of twenty-three coaches and carries **a total of just 104 passengers**. In addition to the coaches intended for socializing and to service carriages for the staff, the rest are completely dedicated to cabins for travelers: each provides for only four passengers, all with luxury services and finishes inspired by the history and culture of Rajasthan, equipped with amenities of all kinds. Each cabin is fitted with air-conditioning, a private bathroom, WiFi, a small refrigerator, cable radio, a safe, a carpet, and much more. Each cabin is also assigned a steward, or a ***khidmutgar***, who is available to passengers day and night. In addition to its luxurious restaurants with international and Indian cuisine, bars, and lounges, the train also has **an Ayurvedic spa**. Daily newspapers and the latest magazines are distributed to passengers each morning.

The Palace on Wheels route is carefully planned to travel its less scenic areas overnight and devote the day both to off-train excursions—as one would on a cruise—and travel through the most beautiful areas of the country. Most meals and breakfasts are also served on board.

The classic itinerary of this prestigious train departs from and arrives at New Delhi after a tour of about 2,450 kilometers (1,522 miles), lasting a total of eight days. It is scheduled for Wednesday in the early afternoon at the station in Delhi, where passengers are welcomed with traditional flower garlands and tikka, a traditional Indian dish of marinated meat cooked on a skewer. They are then accompanied on board to explore the train and see their cabins. The Palace on Wheels leaves the station in the early evening and travels to Jaipur overnight.

On Thursday morning, passengers are welcomed there in a

ceremony with a **royal elephant.** They then visit the Albert Hall Museum, the City Palace, and the UNESCO World Heritage Site of Jaipur's Jantar Mantar, an eighteenth-century astronomical observation site. The off-train excursion continues with a visit to the Hawa Mahal (Palace of Wind) and the Amber Fort, also a UNESCO World Heritage Site. Before passengers reboard the train, there is also time for a tour of the local market.

Very early on Friday morning, passengers get off the train, having arrived the night before at the Sawai Madhopur station for an excursion to the **Ranthambore Tiger Reserve**, which also hosts a rich variety of other wildlife. Later in the morning, the train departs for Chittorgarh, where it arrives in the afternoon, just in time to visit the fort, its history beginning in the eleventh century, considered the largest in all of India.

On Saturday, the fourth day of travel, the train arrives in Udaipur in the morning. There is breakfast on board, then an excursion to the complex of seventeenth-century buildings known as the City Palace, full of towers, domes, and balconies. This is then followed by a boat

176 – A beautiful view of the City Palace and Lake Pichola in Udaipur, Rajasthan.

177 left – The imposing Chittorgarh Fort, showing its fortification walls and the Gaumukh Kund.

177 top right – The Jag Mandir in Udaipur is a palace built on an island in Lake Pichola. It is also called the "Lake Garden Palace."

177 bottom right – A group of tigers early in the morning at Ranthambore National Park, one of the Palace on Wheels' excursion destinations.

ride on Lake Pichola.

Before coming back on board, a visit is scheduled to the royal gardens of Saheliyon-ki-Bari, with some free time for shopping.

On Sunday, the train arrives in Jaisalmer, on the edge of the Thar Desert. It is nicknamed the "City of Gold" due to the color of the sandstone from which it is built. It truly was a city of gold during the medieval period, when it was a strategic hub along **the Silk Road**. The fort, built in the fifteenth century, stands hundreds of meters high above the city of Jaisalmer and shines in the afternoon sun. Passengers also make an excursion to the Sam Sand Dunes in the Thar Desert for a sunset camel ride.

On Monday, the sixth day of the journey, the train stops in the city of Jodhpur to explore the Mehrangarh Fort, built in the sixteenth

178 top – The sun rises and illuminates Mehrangarh Fort and Jaswant Thada cenotaph with the blue city behind.

178 bottom – An Indian camel driver in the dunes of the Thar Desert. The Palace on Wheels also includes a desert excursion by camel.

century atop a rocky hill. Inside the fort complex is a museum with a large, impressive collection of medieval royal clothing and weapons. A visit to the Umaid Bhawan Palace museum follows, then, in the afternoon, the train travels to Bharatpur.

There, at dawn the next morning on the seventh day of travel, travelers visit the Bharatpur Bird Sanctuary, a UNESCO World Heritage Site, and take a rickshaw ride to admire 375 species of local and migratory birds. The train then stops later in the morning at Agra, city of the **Taj Mahal**, and the entire afternoon is dedicated to the masterpiece.

The journey is all but finished, and the next morning, Wednesday at 7:00 a.m., the Palace on Wheels returns to the New Delhi station. This dream has, unfortunately, come to an end.

179 top – The legendary Taj Mahal in Agra, in the Indian state of Uttar Pradesh, is one of this dream train's must-see destinations.

179 bottom – View of the city and fort of Jaisalmer. It is one of the largest, most well-preserved fortified cities in the world and a UNESCO World Heritage Site.

The Darjeeling Himalayan Railway "Toy Train"

In West Bengal, to tourists' amazement, these small blue UNESCO-protected steam locomotives still climb all the way up to Darjeeling.

The **Darjeeling Himalayan Railway**, better known as the **"Toy Train,"** is a wonderful 610-millimeter narrow-gauge railway (about two feet wide) that has run between the cities of New Jalpaiguri and Darjeeling in the Indian state of West Bengal since 1881. It has garnered international celebrity for both its unique route and the beautiful **small blue steam locomotives** that still chug along at the head of its trains. It is now almost completely dedicated to the tourists coming to visit from all around the world. In 1999, the Darjeeling Himalayan Railway, or DHR, as it is commonly called by those in the know, was included on UNESCO's list of World Heritage Sites.

The railway is about 88 kilometers (55 miles) long and climbs from a 100-meter (about 330-foot) altitude in New Jalpaiguri to 2,200 meters (about 7,200 feet) in Darjeeling with an extremely bumpy route. Today the track includes three loops (there used to be five) and four zigzag reverses, which the line uses to quickly gain altitude where there is no space for a normal course. The engineering challenge was to prevent having to build a rack railway, with the technical complications that would have entailed, while also taking into account the relative difficulty acquiring expert personnel for its daily operations. For this reason, it was common to see a worker clinging to the front of the locomotive at the line's steepest stretches s**preading sand on the rails**, especially if they were wet or dirty with leaves, in order to improve the wheels' adhesion.

The route travels almost entirely within the mountains: about 5 kilometers (3 miles) after departure from New Jalpaiguri, the track passes through the line's original terminus of Siliguri, and for another 15 kilometers (9 miles), it proceeds on almost level terrain. From Sukna, the line begins to ascend sharply: up until 1991, there was a

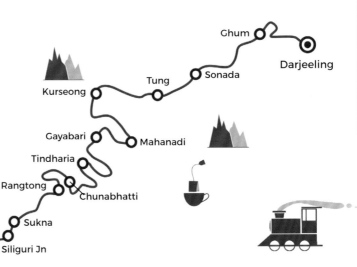

Departure: New Jalpaiguri
Arrival: Darjeeling
Distance: 88 km (55 miles)
Duration: 9 hours
Stages: 1
Country: India – West Bengal

180 – The Darjeeling Himalayan Railway was India's first mountain passenger railroad in 1881. It is a UNESCO World Heritage Site.

180/181 – One of the old "Toy Train" steam locomotives stops at the Darjeeling workshop before resuming service.

 ## PRACTICAL TIPS

THERE ARE TRAINS TO NEW JALPAIGURI FROM ALL ACROSS INDIA. THE MAIN TRAINS FROM KOLKATA ARE THE DAILY "DARJEELING MAIL" NIGHT SERVICE AND THE "SHATABDI EXPRESS" DAY SERVICE (NOT AVAILABLE ON SUNDAYS). FROM NEW DELHI, THE MAIN TRAIN IS THE "RAJDHANI EXPRESS" NIGHT SERVICE (DAILY).

USEFUL WEBSITES

DHR has a modern, easy-to-use online booking system, which can be accessed via **https://www.irctc.co.in/nget/train-search** or through a QR code on the railway's website.

Darjeeling Himalayan Railway: **http://dhr.in.net**

182 – The Batasia Loop near Darjeeling is one of the 360-degree curves that allow the train to move in a circle, gaining altitude within a limited space.

183 – A panoramic view of the city of Darjeeling as seen from the train taking the Batasia Loop. The train stops here to allow passengers to take photographs.

360-degree bend here, "loop 1," which was removed and an alternative route adopted.

After reaching Rongtong, the train confronts its first zigzag, gaining altitude, then, within just 12 kilometers (7.5 miles), overcomes a second loop and two more zigzags. It is one of the most difficult, impressive portions of its journey. It is no coincidence that the loop just traveled is known as **"Agony Point"** and is the tightest curve along the entire track.

In Gayabari, the train is precisely halfway through its journey. Then, after a few kilometers, the train faces the last zigzag and arrives in Kurseong, which also houses the steam locomotive depot and workshops. Here, curiously, the station is at the end of a truncated track that branches off from the main line. When it departs, the train must go into reverse, engaging **a very crowded road intersection** in order to resume its journey to Darjeeling.

After heading through Tung, Sonada, and Rongbull stations, the train arrives in Ghum, which is not only the line's highest point but the highest station in all of India. The station also houses a museum devoted to the railroad. From there, the line descends and faces the Batasia Loop, which is its last, this time downhill. Darjeeling is only 5 kilometers (3 miles) away, and as the train slowly makes its way around the bend in the loop, passengers can see the town further down the valley. Inside the narrow curve stands a memorial dedicated to the Gurkha soldiers of the Indian army. Finally, after about nine hours of travel, the train enters Darjeeling station.

One of the line's main attractions, apart from the track and the magnificent landscape of forests and tea plantations, are the small steam locomotives, painted blue, which still pull some of the tourist trains today (others are entrusted to a more modern, but less glamorous, diesel locomotive). All the steam locomotives are small B-class tank locomotives with only two driving axles, built in the UK between 1889 and 1925. Of the thirty-four delivered to DHR in those years, twelve are still usable. Due to their small size, they almost **look like toy locomotives**, hence the name given to the entire line. Consider that the track is, after all, just 610 millimeters (2 feet) wide, **less than half the standard 1,435-millimeter (4.7-foot) gauge** and just over a third of the broad gauge adopted in 90% of India's network, which is 1,676 millimeters (5.5 feet). Thus, all rolling stock is proportionate to this very narrow track.

Today, the railroad is the destination of thousands upon thousands of tourists each year and has become an important economic resource for the area. Most of the trains running daily are dedicated to tourists, to such a degree that a new panoramic coach has recently been introduced called the **"vistadome" coach**, with large windows on both the sides and the ceiling, inspired by many American and European tourist lines. It is certainly a convenience for passengers but an eyesore when set against the other vintage rolling stock, which make up the train's true charm.

The regular service runs just one train per direction along the entire line, which unfortunately is entrusted to a diesel locomotive. It leaves New Jalpaiguri in the morning and arrives in Darjeeling late afternoon, while in the opposite direction the train leaves Darjeeling a little earlier in the morning to arrive on the plains of New Jalpaiguri earlier in the afternoon. An air-conditioned carriage has also been added to this train, for which the ticket cost has increased slightly, although the price is still affordable.

This train is the successor to the "Darjeeling Mail," DHR's main train that once departed from Siliguri and connected with the broadgauge train of the same name arriving from Kolkata (Sealdah). When Siliguri was just a village, prior to the existence of electronic communications, DHR ensured that mail and newspapers leaving Kolkata (then Calcutta) early in the evening reached Darjeeling

It will not be the same as seeing one in India, but an original Darjeeling Himalayan Railway locomotive, still in operation and restored to its original state, can be seen in the UK. This is the DHR 778, built in 1889, and is the only one that exists outside of India. Number 778 (originally number 19) was built in 1889 by Sharp, Stewart & Co. at the Atlas Works in Glasgow. Since 2009, it has been in service on the Beeches Light Railway, a private railroad in Oxfordshire, but it has also served on the Ffestiniog Railway, the Leighton Buzzard Light Railway, the Launceston Steam Railway, and the South Tynedale Railway. It is the only locomotive of its class to ever be equipped with a small tender.

shortly after noon the next day. Up until the 1980s, this "Darjeeling Mail" operated with two or three sections and transported mail trucks where mail could be distributed to each city along the route.

Since autumn 2021, another (diesel-powered) train called the **Him Kanya** has also been introduced, which runs on Saturdays and Sundays from Darjeeling to Kurseong and back, departing in the morning and returning mid-afternoon, with a stop of about two hours in Kurseong.

On the other hand, travelers who wish to ride on one of the small steam locomotives will need to resort to the tourist services, called **"Joy Rides."** A dozen are run each day, four of them using steam power. These travel only a few kilometers of the line, from Darjeeling to Ghum and back. The complete excursion lasts about two hours, and the route also includes the Batasia Loop, with a short stop to admire Darjeeling from above and view the monument to the Gurkha soldiers. This tourist service is good value for money, although the stream train is a bit more expensive than the diesel train.

There is a third way to travel on this mythical vintage train pulled by the steam locomotive: renting a complete train set (a steam locomotive and two carriages), which costs about 1,000 dollars—affordable, overall, for a small group of travelers, perhaps steam locomotive enthusiasts.

Qinghai-Tibet Railway

The highlands of Tibet and Lhasa seen from the "road to heaven": a train traveling at an altitude of over 4,000 meters (over 13,000 feet) on the highest railway in the world.

Today, they are calling it the **"(rail) road to heaven,"** and there is likely no better nickname for the **Qinghai – Tibet Railway** from Xining, measuring a distance of 1,956 kilometers (1,215 miles). This railroad leads to Lhasa, capital of Tibet, which until 1959 was the residence of the Dalai Lama, the leading spiritual guide of Tibetan Buddhism. It was completed and opened to traffic in 2006, after more than two decades of work in a very difficult environmental context.

The idea for the railroad, however, came much earlier. It is attributed to Mao Zedong, who in 1955 sent a team of technicians to the Tibetan Plateau to evaluate its technical feasibility, which at the time proved to be impossible.

A few numbers give an idea of the size of the undertaking carried out by the Chinese railroad: the 960 kilometers (nearly 600 miles) of this single-track diesel-powered route are over 4,000 meters (over 13,000 feet) high, and the Tanggula station, at 5,068 meters (16,627 feet), is the **highest in the world**, about 200 meters (650 feet) higher than those in the Peruvian Andes. A good 550 kilometers (about 350 miles) of the line run on top of permafrost, which is typical of these altitudes: hard as a stone in winter due to ice, it becomes soft and wet like a swamp in summer, making any kind of construction very difficult. Moreover, the Fenghuoshan Tunnel is the highest railway tunnel in the world, at an altitude of 4,905 meters (16,093 feet). The **lack of oxygen** means that cars needed air-pressure control like an airliner, and special locomotives needed to be built for the harrowing environmental conditions.

Despite these difficulties, the trains travel at 100 kilometers (62 miles) an hour in the section built on permafrost and at

184 – A monument on the observation deck overlooking the Qarhan Salt Plain in the city of Golmud, along the Qinghai – Tibet Railway.

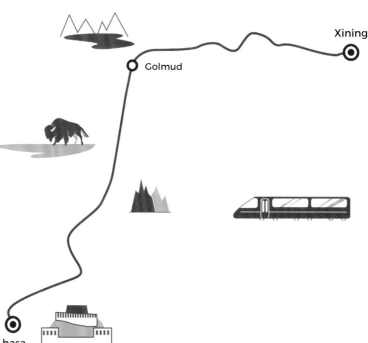

Xining

Golmud

Lhasa

Departure: Xining
Arrival: Lhasa
Distance: 1,956 km (1,215 miles)
Duration: 21 hours
Stages: 1
Country: China

*184/185 – The ultramodern train
bound for Tibet's capital of Lhasa
travels across the highlands amid
the Kunlun Mountains, whose peaks
exceed an altitude of 7,000 meters
(nearly 23,000 feet).*

120 kilometers (75 miles) an hour on the rest of the track.

If these numbers, making the railway truly record-breaking, do not inspire someone to plan a trip on one of its trains, the tracks travel across regions of dazzling beauty that were previously almost impossible to see, and its arrival station is in Lhasa, with its magnificent Potala Palace, the Dalai Lama's chief residence until the Chinese invaded in the 1950s.

For all these reasons, the Qinghai – Tibet Railway has enjoyed great success from its very start, and now millions of travelers have used it in order to discover Tibet and Lhasa. Today, seven major Chinese cities offer **direct trains to Lhasa** from all directions: Beijing in the north, Shanghai in the east, Guangzhou in the south, Chengdu and Chongqing inland, and Xining and Lanzhou in the west. These cities, however, are not the only places that passengers can board a train to Tibet. Trains to Tibet pass through many major cities in China, including Nanjing, Zhengzhou, Xian, Changsha, and Taiyuan.

Xining, however, is the Qinghai – Tibet Railway's true starting

186 top – The Qinghai-Tibet Railway connects Xining to Lhasa, covering nearly 1,000 kilometers (620 miles) at an altitude of over 4,000 meters (13,000 feet).

point, and it is also a point of connection with all other railway lines in greater China. There are two established "trains to Lhasa" departing from Xining stations: **train Z6801**, which gets the green light every morning, and **train Z6811**, which departs in the evening. They respectively reach Lhasa in the morning or evening the day after departure, the journey lasting approximately twenty-one hours.

Train Z6811, departing in the evening, runs only in summertime, when there is a greater influx of tourists. For this reason, the train must also be booked in good time, and, considering that travelers will need to have a travel permit for Tibet added to their Chinese visas, they absolutely must rely on an agency. Visitors attempting to book a train ticket to Lhasa less than thirty days before their scheduled travel date will find it very difficult to get one.

186 bottom – The fascinating Qarhan Salt "Lake," with the city of Golmud standing at its shores.

187 left – One of the numerous bridges and viaducts the Qinghai – Tibet Railway takes as it travels across the rugged, mountainous Tibetan territory toward Lhasa.

187 right – The ultramodern Xining railroad station in the Qinghai region, where the line departs for Lhasa.

The journey aboard this train is very pleasant. To ensure that trains run safely on the Tibetan Plateau, and that passengers travel on board comfortably, all trains for Tibet have been designed to address the conditions of high altitude, low temperature, lack of oxygen, and harsh climate. The main feature of the train to Tibet is its **oxygen supply system**, since, traveling at over 4,000 meters (13,000 feet) high, the flow of oxygen is a key element in ensuring passengers' comfort and safety.

There are two oxygen distribution systems on each train. The first is used to increase the oxygen level inside the train via temperature and air pressure control systems when the train approaches the plateau. The other is available directly to passengers through an independent circuit. Each cabin has oxygen supply tubes and individual oxygen masks for emergencies like those found on airplanes. The carriages, which are very modern, have all the usual services, and a dining car is, of course, also part of the train.

PRACTICAL TIPS

IT IS ALMOST IMPOSSIBLE FOR INDEPENDENT TRAVELERS TO RESERVE AND PURCHASE TICKETS ON THE QINGHAI – TIBET RAILWAY ON THEIR OWN, ESPECIALLY FROM OUTSIDE CHINA. IT IS NECESSARY TO RELY ON AN AGENCY FAMILIAR WITH CHINESE BOOKING METHODS. ONE CAN TAKE A TRAIN TO LHASA DIRECTLY FROM SEVEN MAJOR CHINESE CITIES WITHOUT DEPARTING FROM XINING, BUT THE JOURNEY WILL TAKE LONGER: FORTY HOURS FROM BEIJING, FORTY-SIX HOURS FROM SHANGHAI, AND FIFTY-THREE HOURS FROM GUANGZHOU, FOR EXAMPLE.

USEFUL WEBSITES
https://www.chinahighlights.com/china-trains
https://www.chinatraintickets.net

As for the seats on board, **three different levels of service** are available. The "soft" sleeper berth is very popular, thanks to its spacious, reserved compartment. The soft berth costs about a third more when compared to the "hard" berth, but it also has television screens with headphones and a lockable door, ensuring privacy. The hard sleeper, which, in spite of its name, is as comfortable and soft as the soft sleeper, is smaller (with six per compartment instead of four). There are no screens or headphones, and there is no door to the coach aisle. Even more basic, and inexpensive,

is a simple seat in a car without compartments. Of course, as a tradition on Chinese lines, there is always a kettle full of hot water for tea.

The journey from Xining to Lhasa takes about twenty-four hours, and there is much to see from the windows. Starting from Xining, the first must-see sight is Golmud, a city rising from the Gobi Desert, site of the great **Qarhan Salt Plain**. As the train ascends, travelers arrive at the Yuzhu Peak station at an elevation of 4,160 meters (about 13,650 feet), where, if the weather is

favorable, one can admire the top of Yuzhu Peak before the train enters the Kekexili Nature Reserve. This is an isolated region of the northwestern part of the Tibetan Plateau, and the least populated. Many animals live there, including Tibetan antelopes, wild yaks, and Tibetan wild donkeys.

The train then heads to **the highest point** of the Qinghai – Tibet Railway, Tanggula station. It sits at an altitude of 5,068 meters (16,627 feet), creating the impression of being truly a single step from heaven.

The track enters Nagqu prefecture, and the landscape changes completely. Travelers can admire Tsonag Lake, one of the highest freshwater lakes in China, located a few dozen yards from the railway, which then crosses the vast plains of the Qiangtang basin, one of the five most important pasturelands of the northern Tibetan Plateau, where many rare wild animals live.

Near Damxung station, the prairie is interrupted by the saltwater lake of Namtso, considered sacred by Tibetans. Finally, across a long bridge over the Lhasa River, the train arrives in the **capital of Tibet**, the center of culture for the entire region.

INTERESTING FACTS

It took fifty years to build, but in the end, the highest railway in the world has become a reality. The following are some milestones in its construction. In 1956, the Chinese Ministry of Railways officially started to plan the project, and in the summer of 1957, a team of thirteen people began to perform surveys. In 1958, construction of the Xining – Golmud section began in secret, but works were interrupted several times due to technical and economic issues. In 1974, construction resumed, as did studies for the Golmud – Lhasa section. In September 1979, construction between Xining and Golmud was completed, but the line only opened in 1984. Seventeen years later, in June 2001, construction toward Lhasa began, and the works were completed in October 2005. On July 1, 2006, the Qinghai – Tibet Railway officially came into operation, with tracks on the legendary "road to heaven" finally laid.

188/189 – The celebrated Potala Palace in Lhasa, capital of Tibet. It is named after Mount Potala and was the Dalai Lama's primary residence until 1959.

188 left – UA passenger train in the area of Damxung County in the Tibet Autonomous Region, China.

188 right – A yak on the shores of Lake Namtso on the Tibetan Plateau.

Reunification Express

Traveling from Hanoi to Ho Chi Minh City, on a train that crosses Vietnam each day, between peaceful agricultural lands and places notorious from war in the 1960s.

Following twenty years of war between Vietnam's North and South from 1955 to 1975, a poisonous result of the world's division into two blocs after the Second World War, a railroad became a symbol of the unified country. This is the railroad between Hanoi and Ho Chi Minh City (called Saigon when it was the capital of South Vietnam), which has been dubbed the **Railway of Reunification**. Books and tourist sites, and even the Vietnamese railway site, recount journeys on the **"Reunification Express,"** but a single train with this name does not actually exist.

Five passenger trains per day, however, do run regularly between Hanoi and Ho Chi Minh City (and vice versa), taking about thirty-four hours to travel the long railway's 1,726 kilometers (1,072 miles). These make up the Reunification Express, aboard which travelers can enjoy an experience allowing them to better get to know the Vietnamese while at the same time discovering the country's extraordinary scenery of the sea, jungle, and rice fields, which then gives way to urban areas, teeming like anthills as the train approaches the larger cities.

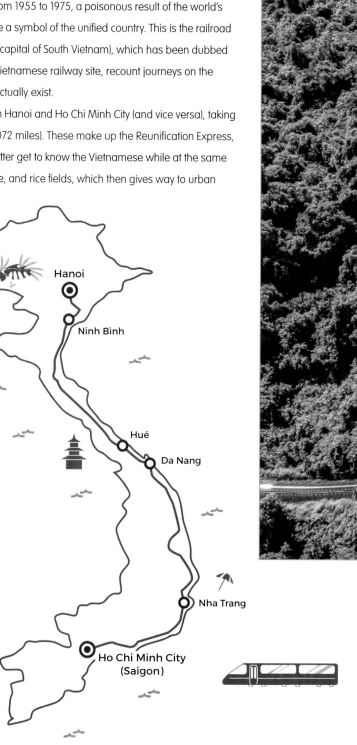

190 – *An incredible image of the train traveling along a street in the Old Quarter of Hanoi. This point on the line in Hanoi is a popular attraction.*

Departure: Hanoi
Arrival: Ho Chi Minh City (Saigon)
Distance: 1,726 km (1,072 miles)
Duration: About 34 hours
Stages: 1
Country: Vietnam

190/191 – The Reunification Express winds its way through the forest on the Hải Vân Pass, in the area of Da Nang.

192 top – Rice fields along the Ngo Dong River in Ninh Bình. Agriculture is still one of Vietnam's chief areas of production.

192 bottom – An aerial view of the train and railroad at Hải Vân Pass on the mountain of Bach Ma, near Hué.

The history of this railway begins in colonial times, when the first miles of track were laid between Hanoi and Vinh in 1899. Construction continued on separate sections until, on October 2, 1936, the entire 1,726-kilometer-long (1,072-mile-long) Hanoi – Saigon connection was officially put into operation. The French, who controlled the entire region, called the railroad the **Transindochinois** ("Trans-Indochinese"). Early connections between the two cities took about the same amount of time as it does today, about forty hours, and the trains were chiefly intended for Europeans living in the country. The trains were luxurious, with comfortable sleeping cars and a restaurant, even a **movie room and a hairdresser**.

Times of luxury and wealth did not last long, however, and, with the outbreak of World War II, French Indochina was invaded by Japanese troops. The railroad soon became a target of sabotage by the Viet Minh resistance and allied bombings, and it was heavily damaged. After the Second World War, the First Indochina War broke out, and the railway again became the object of Viet Minh **sabotage**, this time against the French.

With the signing of the 1954 Geneva Conference agreements, the French left Vietnam, and the country was split in two: North Vietnam, controlled by a Communist government, and South Vietnam, led by a U.S.-backed pro-Western government. The **railroad line was split in two** at Hiên Lương Bridge, over the Bến Hải River in Quảng Tri Province.

With the outbreak of hostilities between the two Vietnams and direct U.S. intervention in the conflict from 1964, both the north and south lines were heavily damaged. In the north, it was American bombings that disabled the tracks, and in the south, sabotage by the Vietcong. It is a strange feeling, today, to travel along the line surrounded by lovely, peaceful landscape and ask oneself how much violence and tragedy

193 left – In the main square of Hanoi's Old Quarter, rickshaw drivers take tourists around the city.

193 right – A glimpse of the Imperial City of Huế, a fortified complex of palaces and temples that was once the emperor's residence.

played out along the track.

Saigon fell on April 30, 1975—illustrated by the iconic photo of the final helicopter taking off from the roof of the U.S. Embassy—and the new unified Vietnam's Communist government **reconnected the two halves** of the railway line, which, unfortunately, was very damaged. Many numbers circulate concerning the bridges, stations, and switches repaired within a short time by the new railroad administration—all data that is difficult to verify. Certainly, an enormous effort was made to get the line back into operation as quickly as possible along its entire route, both for economic purposes and for more than understandable political reasons.

Connecting Hanoi by rail to Saigon, renamed Ho Chi Minh City, in a mainly agricultural country with extremely difficult roads, was a sign of the country's unity and a symbol of victory following twenty years of war. Traveling these rails today means not only interacting with the timeline of these significant events, but also the religious and cultural divisions between the Catholic north with its French history, and the Buddhist south, influenced by American culture.

The railway, despite its punishing structural limitations—the narrow

PRACTICAL TIPS

THOSE WISHING TO MAKE STOPS IN CITIES ALONG THE TRAIN ROUTE WILL NEED TO BOOK SEPARATE TICKETS, WITH RESERVATIONS FOR EACH ROUTE BEING TRAVELED. IN VIETNAM, MOTORCYCLES AND MOPEDS ARE VERY COMMON, AND THEY CAN BE BROUGHT ONTO THE TRAIN BY PAYING FOR A SPECIAL TICKET. IT IS ADVISABLE TO BRING FOOD ALONG ON THIS TRIP, ALTHOUGH A REFRESHMENT SERVICE WITH VIETNAMESE FOOD COOKED TO ORDER IS AVAILABLE ON BOARD, WHICH IS ALWAYS VERY ATTRACTIVE AND AFFORDABLE.

USEFUL WEBSITES
Vietnam Railways:
http://vietnam-railway.com/train/SapaTourist /reunification-express-train

The Imperial City of Huế is a complex of monumental buildings that UNESCO recognized as a World Heritage Site in 1993. Its construction began in 1804, after Nguyễn Ánh ascended the throne in June 1789, having proclaimed himself emperor and chosen his clan's ancestral seat, the town of Huế, to be the capital. The complex, built facing the Perfume River, is square and features a configuration of concentric squares. The fortified ramparts are 2 kilometers (1.2 miles) long and surrounded by a moat. Within these walls are a series of courtyards, palaces, and pavilions. The complex was the seat of imperial power until the 1880s, with the imposition of the French protectorate. It then remained the symbolic center of the monarchy up until the end of the Nguyen dynasty in 1945 and the Democratic Republic of Vietnam's Proclamation of Independence that same year.

gauge, bridges, tunnels, and a maximum speed of just 50 kilometers (about 30 miles) an hour—plays a fundamental role in connecting the country's north and south, given that more than 85% of all passenger traffic and 60% of freight on the entire Vietnamese railroad network take place on this line.

A trip on one of the five daily express trains connecting Hanoi and Ho Chi Minh City (which locals still call Saigon) offers an interesting insight into the country. The train departs Hanoi at a walking pace among the suburban **houses, built just over a meter from the track**. From their window, passengers can see people's rooms, women cooking, teens watching television or lying on their bed, or a hairdresser at work. Dozens upon dozens of scooters and bicycles lean against walls in the narrow space between the train and the buildings. Some of the hanging laundry risks getting caught on the train cars.

Once in the open countryside, the landscape alternates between rice fields and areas of spontaneous, lush vegetation. It conveys a pleasant feeling of tranquility, a contrast with Hanoi's incessant noise of mopeds, horns, and chaos.

The route stops at some interesting places, which can provide excellent opportunities to interrupt the journey and break it up into two or three stages. From north to south, the train stops at Ninh Bình, 93 kilometers (58 miles) south of Hanoi and the capital of a rural area known for its spectacular karst reliefs, caves, temples, and waterways; Huế, the ancient capital of Vietnam with its **splendid Imperial City**, rich in history and culture; and Da Nang, a modern city on the coast where pagodas and Buddhist temples intermingle with beaches and entertainment. From here, one can reach the stunning Hộ i An by bus or taxi. Various eras and architectural styles coexist in this city, ranging from temples and Chinese wooden shophouses to colorful French colonial buildings, to sophisticated Vietnamese "tube houses"

194 – The splendor of illuminated boats in front of the ancient city of Hội An, a UNESCO World Heritage Site, in the province of Quảng Nam.

195 left – The spectacular Dragon Bridge in Da Nang, illuminated by the light of the setting sun.

195 top right – Ho Chi Minh City Hall, or the Ho Chi Minh City People's Committee Head Office, built from 1902 to 1908 in the French colonial style for what then was the city of Saigon.

195 bottom right – A quiet beach in the natural paradise of Nha Trang. Here, wartime is a distant memory.

and the famous Japanese bridge, covered by a pagoda. Finally, before reaching Ho Chi Minh City, passengers might stop at Nha Trang, the country's best-known seaside resort. Vietnamese trains are no Orient Express (as the state railways' website explains with a pinch of self-deprecation), but the quality of service on board is good, with the usual features of Asian long-distance trains. There are, then, two classes of seats, "hard" and "soft" (the former with wooden benches, the second with bus-style seats) and two classes of berth, here also distinguished as a Hard or Soft Sleeper. The first has six berths per compartment, and the second has only four, which are a little larger—most importantly, the cabin space is shared between four rather than six people. The price difference is only a few dollars, so the Soft Berth is certainly recommended. Finally, the fifth option is a so-called VIP Berth, a compartment with only two beds, ideal for couples traveling together.

Tiger Express

The beautiful luxury train traveling between the ultramodern city-state of Singapore and the Thai capital of Bangkok, raising funds to save the world's remaining wild tigers.

As of autumn 2019, the **"Tiger Express"** is the new name of the **Eastern & Oriental Express**, a luxury tourist train operating mainly (but not solely) on the line between Singapore and Bangkok. The prominent tour operator Belmond Management Ltd., owner of this train—in addition to the Orient Express—has joined the British organization **Save Wild Tigers** in support of a global campaign to protect the last remaining wild tigers in the world. Up to 20% of the Tiger Express ticket price is donated to the organization for this cause aiming to save the magnificent feline from extinction, with no more than 3,800 of them remaining in the wild.

The train was decorated inside and out with tiger-inspired works by the Chinese pop artist Jacky Tsai. Apart from these intriguing new additions, the train has been one of the most celebrated, luxurious tourist trains in all of Southeast Asia since 1993, with the quality of the service offered and the allure of its carriages undoubtedly placing it at the level of a grand five-star hotel. The train is composed of Japanese-built carriages from the 1970s, which originally were briefly used on New Zealand's Silver Star train, with interiors now completely redone with furnishings inspired by the colonial era.

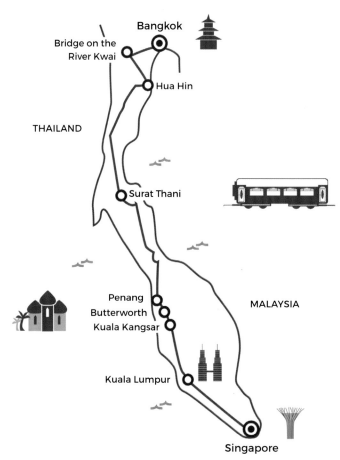

Departure: Singapore
Arrival: Bangkok
Distance: 1,503 km (934 miles)
Duration: 3 days/2 nights
Stages: 1
Country: Singapore, Malaysia, Thailand

196 top – The Tiger Express stopping at Bangkok's Hua Lamphong station.

196 bottom – The plush interior of a compartment on the Tiger Express.

196/197 – Aboard the Tiger Express luxury train, passengers travel through Thailand and Malaysia's lush tropical vegetation.

198 top – The opulent Tiger Express passes by a traditional paddy field, with many rice farm workers bending over, knee-deep in the water.

198 bottom – Sunrise at the Singapore Marina with its landmark monument, the Merlion.

The Tiger Express travels once or twice a month between Singapore and Bangkok from March to December, but the service does add other itineraries stopping at further locations in the region. The duration of the journey, on about 1,500 kilometers (930 miles) of narrow meter-gauge, single-track railroad line, is three days, with two nights aboard inside the train's luxurious sleeping compartments.

Departure is scheduled for mid afternoon from Singapore Woodlands Train Checkpoint. This is the Asian city-state's border station, located at the south end of the Johor-Singapore Causeway, the island's first road and rail link with Malaysia built in 1923. Arrival at the monumental station in Kuala Lumpur, capital of Malaysia, is scheduled for just before midnight.

On the second day, the train stops for a couple of hours in Kuala Kangsar, then continues its journey through the tropical forest and giant tea plantations toward the famous Kwae Yai Bridge. A stop is scheduled there, on the morning of the third day, for a short boat trip under the bridge. Following a stop in Kanchanaburi, at a station about 5 kilometers (3 miles) from the bridge, the train resumes its journey and, after a final leg of about 130 kilometers (80 miles), arrives in Bangkok at the magnificent Hua Lamphong station, which was inaugurated in 1916.

One feature of the Tiger Express is its observation car at the end of the train. This is a lounge car that is **half open-air**, like a ship's deck, allowing passengers to further appreciate the landscape, enjoying both the colors and the scents of the areas being crossed: this is a great spot for taking photographs and for quality video recording. Apart from this car, one of its most popular and sought-after, the Tiger Express also has two dining cars in its lineup, a bar car with piano, and a second lounge car for onboard socializing.

PRACTICAL TIPS

THE TRIP IS ALSO OFFERED IN THE OPPOSITE DIRECTION, FROM BANGKOK TO SINGAPORE.

USEFUL WEBSITES
Eastern & Oriental Express:
https://www.belmond.com/it/trains/asia/eastern-and-oriental-express

Tiger Express:
https://www.belmond.com/ideas/articles/on-the-trail-of-the-tiger

The Save Wild Tigers Association:
https://www.savewildtigers.org

The Tiger Express has three types of sleeping compartments on board with varying configurations, and, of course, proportionate costs. The Pullman cabin is the simplest, with a folding table and a sofa, which a steward will convert into two comfortable berths during dinner. It also includes a small bathroom with a toilet, shower, and sink. Alternatively, passengers can select a State sleeping cabin about double the size of the Pullman, with **two berths that are side by side**, rather than one above the other. There is a sofa, lounge seat, and a chair, with two large windows rather than one. The bathroom is similar to the Pullman cabin's, and the car's steward also converts these compartments to their nighttime setup during dinner. Finally, the third option is one of two Presidential suites. These have a similar layout to the standard sleeping cabins but with much more space. The bathroom in these two very luxurious cabins is also larger than the others, even though it features the same setup. The materials, colors, and design of all the furnishings reference the colonial period of the late nineteenth and early twentieth century.

INTERESTING FACTS

During World War II, the Japanese used Allied POWs to build a railway from Thailand to Burma. This was so they could supply their army, without the dangers of shipping supplies by sea. Many prisoners died under the terrible conditions, to such a degree that the line came to be known as the "Death Railway." David Lean's epic 1957 film *The Bridge on the River Kwai* centers on one of the line's major engineering works, the Kwae Yai River Bridge north of Kanchanaburi. The film was shot in Sri Lanka, but the River Kwai Bridge is real and still used by local passenger trains from Bangkok to Nam Tok. For anyone interested in twentieth-century history, a visit to Kanchanaburi and the infamous "Death Railway" is a must.

199 left – The Tiger Express crosses the Bridge on the River Kwai, a well-known site in the history of the Second World War.

199 right – Bangkok's golden Grand Palace stands out against the city's large, modern skyscrapers at sunrise.

The Stove Train

Departure: Goshogawara
Arrival: Tsugaru-Nakasato
Distance: 20 km (12 miles)
Duration: 45 minutes
Stages: 1
Country: Japan

The "Stove Train" between Goshogawara and the Tsugaru-Nakasato station in Aomori Prefecture's freezing winter, revealing a traditional, authentic Japan.

Japan, land of high-speed trains, where a prototype of the latest **Maglev bullet train** recently exceeded 600 kilometers (370 miles) per hour, holds a small, old train as a precious relic, traveling the **Tsugaru railroad** track at 50 kilometers (about 30 miles) per hour in the prefecture of Aomori. This small train is universally known as the **"Stove Train."**

During winter in this frigid area, snowfalls of up to 5 meters (over 16 feet) are not uncommon. This is when a couple of old heated carriages are hitched to the usual diesel railcar that runs daily between Goshogawara and Tsugaru-Nakasato, traveling along the 20 kilometers (12 miles) of narrow-gauge railroad (1,067 millimeters, or 3.5 feet, wide). Each of the heated cars features two antique cast-iron **stoves** on which railway workers and travelers grill pieces of *surume* (dried squid and cuttlefish), as well as rice cakes and rice balls. Born as a rural railroad serving the twelve towns on its itinerary, the line has turned into an international tourist attraction, as well as a social event and ritual for the Japanese, who take part in large numbers.

The Stove Train is actually just one, though certainly the most famous and exciting, of the events that the railroad offers throughout the year, linked to Japanese traditions and a great passion for nature. In summer, the railway runs a *furin* train (*furin* being Japanese bells that sound when the wind blows): the wind-chime bells are hung from the ceilings of all the trains in service alongside strips of haiku written by locals. In autumn, the *suzumushi* (cricket) train is

200 – Passengers warm themselves next to a coal stove on the Tsugaru Railway's Stove Train in Goshogawara, in Japan's Aomori Prefecture.

201 – A Tsugaru Railway Stove Train travels through the snow. The trains featuring coal stoves in the coaches have become a tourist attraction.

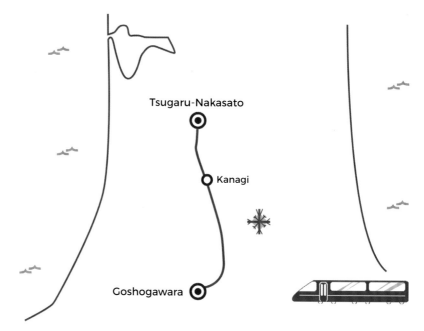

Tsugaru-Nakasato

Kanagi

Goshogawara

PRACTICAL TIPS

THE CLOSEST AIRPORT TO GOSHOGAWARA IS IN AOMORI, WHICH IS ABOUT FORTY MINUTES AWAY BY CAR. ONE CAN ARRIVE VIA A TRAIN, OF COURSE, FROM THE EAST JAPAN RAILWAY COMPANY. THE TSUGARU RAILWAY STATION IS NEARBY.

USEFUL WEBSITES
Official website (in Japanese): **https://tsutetsu.com**

Goshogawara City tourist website (in English):
https://www.city.goshogawara.lg.jp/tourism/en/view/tsutetsu.html

Aomori Prefecture:
http://www.tsugarunavi.jp/en/detail/03_004_goshogawara_a.html

organized. The wind chimes are replaced with baskets housing *suzumushi*, Asian crickets that are raised as pets in Japan. Ashino Park (near Ashino Park station) is another popular spot during cherry blossom season that can be reached by train.

The Tsugaru Railway Company was founded in 1928, and the first section of the line was inaugurated on July 15, 1930, running from Goshogawara to Kanagi. The section was extended to Ōzawanai on October 4, 1930, and to the present-day terminus of Tsugaru-Nakasato on November 13, 1930. It is the northernmost private railway line in Japan. Kanagi is the only transfer station on the entire line, with circulation managed via a staff token system.

The Stove Train is what made Tsugaru Railway famous, running several times each day from December 1 to March 31 each year. On days when the snow is particularly heavy, a diesel locomotive equipped with a **snowplow** is added to the front of the train. To access the cars with coal stoves, travelers must pay a higher fee than the price of riding in a normal railcar, which remains in the train's setup. The cars have a basic setup: on each side of the corridor is a row of seats facing each other, with an old table in the center. The rows of seats on both right and left sides are interrupted by two old cast-iron stoves, placed a certain distance from each other to distribute heat throughout the carriage. These are charcoal fired, round cast-iron stoves traditionally called "Daruma stoves." This is because their stout shapes are said to be reminiscent of Daruma dolls, iconic Japanese figures inspired by the posture of the Zen patriarch Bodhidharma while in seated meditation. On top of each stove is a grill, and a chimney pipe behind it; these rise in two curves, emerging through the roof.

INTERESTING FACTS

The train experience is first-rate in Japan, so travelers are likely to make other trips apart from the Tsugaru Railway. The Japan Rail Pass may be of interest, permitting travel over seven, fourteen, or twenty-one consecutive days on almost all the trains of the Japan Railways (JR) Group—the company contains Japan's seven major railways, including the East Japan Railway, which serves the city of Goshogawara. The Japan Rail Pass, designed to work like Europe's Interrail pass, is very convenient for those traveling around the country, but it does not make sense for visitors staying a week in Tokyo or another city. It does not cover subway or bus transportation, nor does it include many private local railways. Travelers must purchase the pass before they leave for Japan, either online at www.Jrailpass.com or at certain agencies in major cities.

As soon as the ride has begun, passengers hand the two conductors on board their pieces of calamari and cuttlefish to be grilled on the stoves, which are occasionally fueled with pieces of coal. The temperature is pleasant, with the undulating rural landscape, often covered with snow flows, rolling past the windows. Rail workers also pass through the wagon pushing an old metal cart selling bags of dried squid and locally brewed sake.

The Stove Train takes passengers on a journey through time. It offers passengers a sense of nostalgia for a world that is now becoming more and more difficult to find in a Japan famous for its technological advances and ultramodern cities. The journey takes about forty-five minutes, and once in Tsugaru-Nakasato, waiting for the return journey, travelers can enjoy a special chicken and vegetable soup called *tsutetsujiru* just outside the station. It can definitely be said that this train is *megoi*, a term in local dialect meaning "adorable and very small."

202 – The Tsugaru Railway train connects Goshogawara and Tsugaru-Nakasato over a distance of 20 kilometers (12 miles).

203 left – Winter is very cold on the Tsugaru Railway, the very reason it has turned into an unusual tourist attraction.

203 right – A Tsugaru Railway worker inspects the connection between coaches before the Stove Train departs for Goshogawara.

The Ghan

Following the tracks of "Afghan" cameleers: on a rail to the Australian Outback and across the entire continent, from Adelaide in the south to Darwin in the north.

The Ghan is a luxury tourist train offering a dream journey on Australia's intercontinental rail line from Adelaide to Darwin. It is managed by Journey Beyond Rail Expeditions, part of the Journey Beyond group, a leader in the tourism sector that also provides other luxury train services within Australia. The Ghan runs along a legendary railway that crosses the formidable Australian desert from south to north, allowing passengers to explore some of the most beautiful areas of the country—areas they would not have gotten to know so well on a flight.

"Ghan" is short for "Afghan." Today's train is named after an historic twentieth-century train, then dubbed the "Afghan Express," which penetrated the country's interior via an early narrow-gauge railway. The first people to create a path through the Australian desert were reputedly "Afghan" **cameleers**, though many of the people labeled "Afghan" at the time were from areas south of today's Afghanistan, including parts of present-day Pakistan. In any case, the legend still persists about their journey across the desert between Australia's south and north coasts, and the Ghan embodies it perfectly.

Construction of the first railroad began in Port Augusta in 1878. It ran to Oodnadatta, where the track arrived in January 1891. Works were halted until 1926, when the line was extended in the direction of Alice Springs, a major city in the **Australian Outback**, reaching the city in 1929.

204 – The Ghan offers various levels of service: this is the train's comfortable Platinum Service sleeping compartment.

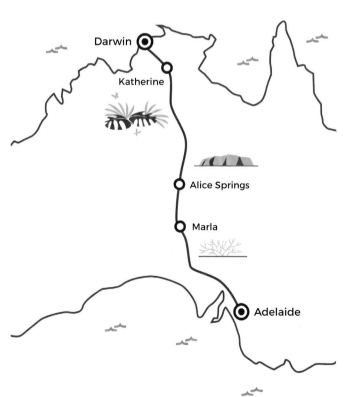

Departure: Adelaide
Arrival: Darwin
Distance: 2,979 km (1,851 miles)
Duration: 54 hours
Stages: 1 or 2 of your choice
Country: Australia

204/205 – A stunning drone image of the Ghan at full speed in the Australian Outback. The journey from Adelaide to Darwin is 2,979 kilometers (1,851 miles) long.

There was a clear intention to continue northward to Darwin, but nothing was built, and camel drivers, Afghan or otherwise, continued to drive their camel trains from Alice Springs to the north coast. The track had moreover been laid without adequate geological studies and was always subject to **flood and landslides**, further disadvantaging the service.

In the 1970s, it was finally decided that a new line—a modern, cross-continental backbone—was to be constructed. A new route was created, also single-track but now with a standard gauge, about 160 kilometers (about 100 miles) west of the old track, connecting Alice Springs in the interim. The line was inaugurated in October 1980, and shortly afterward, the old narrow-gauge line was abandoned. The line again stopped short of continuing to Darwin,

however, as a new government canceled the project. It remained frozen until 1999, when the AustralAsia Rail Corporation was finally commissioned to build and manage the 1,420-kilometer (about 880-mile) stretch between Alice Springs and Darwin. Construction began in July 2001 and was completed, in record time, in September 2003.

On February 4, 2004, the first passenger train arrived in Darwin, having departed from Adelaide forty-seven hours earlier. The southern and northern coasts were finally connected by rail, 113 years after its first section was constructed.

The Ghan crosses many varied landscapes on its long journey, all of them incredibly beautiful. The green hills of South Australia gradually give way to the desert of Australia's wild Outback. Then, the tracks cross the "Red Centre" (as the Alice Springs area is popularly named, due to its bold coloring), a few miles from **Uluru/Ayers Rock**. The train finally arrives in the rainforest in Australia's Top End, the northernmost part of the Northern Territory, in all its tropical splendor.

PRACTICAL TIPS

THE GHAN DOES NOT TRAVEL IN DECEMBER OR JANUARY. THOUGH ONE MIGHT EXPECT THE INTERIOR OF AUSTRALIA TO ALWAYS BE VERY HOT, TEMPERATURES CAN DROP TO AS LOW AS 5°C (41°F) IN THE EARLY MORNING AND EVENING, SO IT IS ALSO NECESSARY TO BRING APPROPRIATE CLOTHING. THERE IS NO DRESS CODE TO FOLLOW WHILE ABOARD THE TRAIN.

USEFUL WEBSITES
The Ghan:
https://www.journeybeyondrail.com.au/the-ghan

206 – The Ghan near Marla station in the middle of the Australian Outback, amid its characteristic red soil dotted with shrubs.

207 left – An aerial view of the skyline in Alice Springs from the Anzac Hill Memorial lookout, showing the main buildings of the city's center.

207 right – Passengers on the Ghan visit an old quarry in the isolated East MacDonnell Ranges for a special memorial event.

INTERESTING FACTS

Those looking to experience the thrill of the century-old Afghan Express, complete with a steam locomotive and vintage cars, can take a ride on the Pichi Richi Railway, a heritage railway that has been restored and put back into service on a 78-kilometer (48-mile) stretch of the original narrow-gauge line between Port Augusta and Quorn. The railroad, which has been operated by the Pichi Richi Railway Preservation Society since 1973, is in service from March to November. Its NM25 is one of the original Afghan Express locomotives pulling the set, which also includes some wooden carriages from the 1920s. Port Augusta is located about 300 kilometers (190 miles) north of Adelaide and is easily accessed via Highway 1 (route A1). The heritage railway's website is https://www.pichirichirailway.org.au.

208 top – A lovely view of Katherine Gorge in Nitmiluk National Park, in Australia's Northern Territory.

208 bottom – The Pichi Richi Railway's tourist steam train crosses a bridge in the Flinders Ranges near Quorn.

The train heads north once a week, departing Sunday around midday from Adelaide station and arriving in Darwin on Tuesday late afternoon. In the opposite direction, departure from Darwin is on Wednesday morning, arriving in Adelaide on Friday early afternoon.

Along the journey are two stops in addition to Alice Springs. The first is in the afternoon on the second day of travel at Marla, 400 kilometers (about 250 miles) south of Alice Springs, **a remote outpost** in the Outback where visitors can immerse themselves deep in the Australian interior. The small village has about 100 inhabitants and was officially recognized by the government in May 1981 as "a base for the **provision of essential services** to travellers crossing the continent." Marla has a health center, the Marla Clinic, run on behalf of the state government by the Royal Flying Doctor Service of Australia (volunteer doctors who, as the name implies, travel via helicopter across the huge Australian desert), a regional police station, and a privately owned complex called Marla Travellers Rest, described as consisting of a roadhouse, hotel and motel, restaurant, service station, supermarket, and caravan (trailer) park. A sign at the town's entrance reads: "Welcome to the most remote Australia!"

The Ghan's next stop of Alice Springs, a town of 25,000 inhabitants, seems like a metropolis in comparison. Here, in addition to visiting the city, visitors have the option of taking a helicopter ride, a very common means of transportation in Australia's interior (used by cattle breeders to follow and guide their herds, for example). The stop in this city, nearly halfway between Adelaide and Darwin, lasts four and a half hours.

The train then departs, heading northward and making a stop the next morning in Katherine, 320 kilometers (about 200 miles) from Darwin. Here in the Northern Territory, the landscape has changed, and passengers are now on the border between the Outback desert and the **tropical forest** of Australia's far north. The city is spread along the Katherine River, and a hike to the Nitmiluk Gorge in Nitmiluk National Park is part of the itinerary. After fifty-four hours of travel and adventure, the long train—thirty-six cars, 774 meters (half a mile) long altogether—enters Darwin station. The station is about 18 kilometers (11 miles) from the city center and is still quite spartan, in part because the Ghan is the only passenger service terminating there.

Travelers can also cross the continent in the opposite direction,

of course, and they can also cut the tour in half, riding the Ghan between either Adelaide or Darwin and Alice Springs.

Passengers can choose from three levels of service. A Gold Service twin cabin provides a three-seater lounge that converts into upper and lower berths and a compact private bathroom with sink, toilet, and shower, as well as retractable tables and reading lamps. The Gold Service single cabin has similar features to the twin cabin, including a wash basin, but the toilets and showers are at the end of the car.

All Gold Service cabins come with a welcome kit, complimentary bath towels, and toiletry. Passengers looking for more space and additional comfort can choose one of the two Gold Superior Service cabins, featuring a double bed and fold-down upper berth, as well as a private lounge with a DVD player, a table, armchairs, and a mini bar. At an even higher level, Platinum Service offers a package that, in addition to a private cabin, includes all meals, all standard alcoholic and nonalcoholic drinks, off-train excursions and Outback experiences, and a private transfer service to and from the train station.

209 top – The Ghan's railroad line crosses the Stuart Highway, in an image offering an idea of Australia's vast space.

209 bottom – Ghan passengers on a hike in Katherine Gorge in Nitmiluk National Park.

AUSTRALIA
ADELAIDE TO BRISBANE

Departure: Adelaide
Arrival: Brisbane
Distance: 2,000 km (1,242 miles)
Duration: Approximately 56 hours
Stages: 2
Country: Australia

210/211 – The Great Southern tourist train travels across the verdant landscape near Nana Glen, a town near Coffs Harbour in New South Wales.

Great Southern

Two days discovering the lush, sunny coasts of South Australia between Adelaide, Canberra, and Brisbane.

The **Great Southern** is the latest addition among Australia's long-distance luxury tourist trains. It travels only in the summer months (in the Southern Hemisphere) of December and January between Adelaide, Canberra, and Brisbane. The route is about 2,000 kilometers (1,242 miles), which differs somewhat depending on the direction of travel. Like the more well-known "Ghan," it is managed by Journey Beyond Rail Expeditions. The trip lasts three days, with two nights aboard the train, and includes three off-train excursions to visit some areas surrounding the route. There are no sunny deserts here, nor remote wastelands: the Great Southern takes passengers along the rugged **coastline of South Australia** amid sun-kissed beaches and cities teeming with energy and entertainment, all with the luxury and comfort now customary on such trains.

In the two months that it operates, the train has sixteen scheduled departures (eight in each direction) from South Australia, arriving in Queensland after traveling across Victoria, New South Wales, and the Australian Capital Territory. This trip is only possible on the Great Southern, not only for the quality of the service offered, but for the lack of passenger rail connections along the route. Australians not traveling for pleasure prefer to fly long-distance, but here, passengers rediscover the allure of slow rail travel, when the arrival time at one's destination is less important than the experience aboard the train and what was seen and discovered out the window—things that could not have been observed from a small window 10,000 meters (33,000 feet) above the ground.

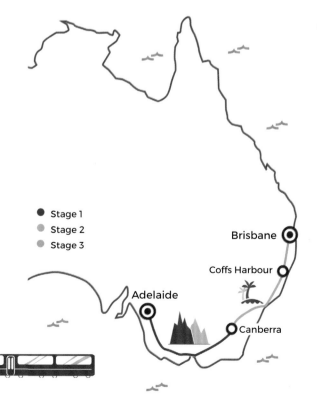

Stage 1
Stage 2
Stage 3

Brisbane
Coffs Harbour
Adelaide
Canberra

211 – The comfortable dining car reserved for Platinum Service aboard the Great Southern.

212 top – The modern architecture of Adelaide's city center.

212 bottom – Boroka Lookout in Grampians National Park, Victoria, Australia.

Australian luxury trains are experiencing a significant increase in passengers, both international and domestic, attracted to the unique beauty of the regions traveled, and to the trains' impeccably organized tours. The Great Southern's set consists of twenty-eight coaches and can carry up to 214 passengers. Unlike the Ghan, whose two diesel locomotives at the front are painted red with a stylized camel design, this train has a kangaroo for its logo and is entrusted to a pair of diesel locomotives painted a pleasant sienna, a reference to the color of the beaches, warmed by the setting sun.

The eastbound train departs from Adelaide on Friday morning. As passengers settle into their cabins and sip a cocktail before sitting down to lunch in the sumptuous dining car, the train makes its way to the Grampian mountains area, about 460 kilometers (about 290 miles) from Adelaide. There, passengers take their first excursion, a guided bus tour through the charming town of Halls Gap, located in Grampians National Park and an ideal base for exploring this spectacular corner of Australia. From Halls Gap, passengers continue to the Boroka Lookout to take in a view of the eastern Grampians and the city lying at the bottom of the valley. Passengers can reach two viewing platforms in a five-minute walk, where they can view the nearby Lake Bellfield. Alternatively, alongside an expert guide, visitors can hike the Venus Baths Loop Walk from Halls Gap. This relaxing walk of two and a half kilometers (about a mile and a half) crosses Stony Creek, immersing hikers in the peace and tranquility of nature. The deepest rock pools hold water even in the summer months.

Those more interested in food and wine can opt for a visit to the Seppelt Winery, which offers wines from four different vineyards in three different grape-growing regions. This ensures an engaging experience of Australian wine, with a private tasting followed by a tour through the winery's tunnels and underground cellars. Passengers reboard the train to head to Canberra, making a long stop on the second day of the trip for a comprehensive visit to the nation's political capital. The train stops at Yass Junction station, where passengers are transferred by bus to Parliament House for a sumptuous lunch in the Great Hall and then an in-depth tour of the building and its halls. In the afternoon, a visit is scheduled to the Australian War Memorial, a moment for reflection and remembrance of the Australians who sacrificed their lives for freedom and democracy around the world. Finally, prior to boarding again at Goulburn station, there is time for a tour of the National Portrait Gallery.

As passengers have dinner on board and retire to their comfortable cabins, the train continues toward Brisbane, but not before it makes a stop on the morning of the third day in Coffs Harbour, a lively tourist and commercial center, and one of the most beautiful cities in New South Wales. A coach takes travelers to the Great Divide, a 3,500-kilometer-long (over 2,100-mile-long) mountain range. Here, on the edge of the rainforest, the Sealy Lookout is home to the Forest Sky Pier, a viewing platform that towers atop a hill with breathtaking views. Back in the city, visitors receive a guided tour of the North Coast Regional Botanic Garden, which spans over 20 hectares (50 acres), dedicated to exotic plants from the world's subtropical regions. Alternatively, there are two other excursions available, one an 8-kilometer (5-mile) cycling tour to an estuary called North Point Lookout, where visitors can enjoy a magnificent view of the Solitary Islands and the surrounding Marine Park. There is, however, a perfectly attractive opportunity for lazier passengers, since a magnificent beach lies directly next to Urunga station, where they can relax completely while strolling by the sea.

PRACTICAL TIPS

THE BRISBANE – ADELAIDE ITINERARY FOLLOWS A SLIGHTLY DIFFERENT ROUTE AND OFFERS SHORE EXCURSIONS AT DIFFERENT LOCATIONS, WITH THE EXCEPTION OF THE COFFS HARBOUR STOP. INSTEAD, IT INCLUDES A VISIT TO HUNTER VALLEY WINE COUNTRY AND THE CITY OF MELBOURNE, RATHER THAN CANBERRA.

USEFUL WEBSITES
The Great Southern:
https://www.journeybeyondrail.com.au/great-southern/great -southern-experience

213 top – Kangaroos poke around on the beautiful beach in Coffs Harbour.

213 bottom – Excellent wines are produced in Australia's southeast: pictured here, the Peter Seppelt Winery in the Barossa Valley.

Around lunchtime, passengers get back on the train to head to Brisbane, where their arrival is expected late in the afternoon.

The journey is full of exciting and curious sights, but just as rewarding is the experience aboard the train, thanks to its masterfully curated cabins, which stewards on board convert from a day- to night-time setup while passengers have dinner in the dining car. Three levels of service are available, two of which include a double or single cabin. The Gold Service twin cabin features a lounge that converts into two berths, one above the other, and a private bathroom with a sink, toilet, and shower, as well as retractable tables and reading lamps. The Gold Service single cabin has similar features to the double cabin, including the sink, but with toilets and showers located at the far end of the carriages. All Gold Service cabins include a welcome kit, along with toiletry bags. Passengers who desire additional space and comfort can select the Gold Superior cabins, which feature a double bed and fold-down upper berth, as well as a private lounge with DVD player, table, armchairs, and a mini bar. Finally, the Platinum Service offers a package that, in addition to a private cabin, includes meals and all drinks, off-train excursions, and private transfers to and from the train station.

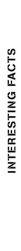

Whether to travel from Adelaide to Brisbane or vice versa is no easy decision, especially since the two itineraries stop at different cities: Canberra in the first instance, and Melbourne the second. The stop in Victoria's state capital makes up a full day's schedule, which, in addition to an ascent to the Melbourne Skydeck (the highest public observation deck in the Southern Hemisphere at a height of 297 meters, or 975 feet) and a tour on the banks of the Yarra River, includes stops at the Melbourne Cricket Ground, the historic Flinders Street railroad station, and Port Phillip Bay. The visit includes lunch at the popular 5-star restaurant Eureka 89, featuring dishes based on seasonal produce, accompanied by wines from all across Australia.

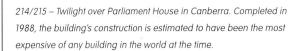

214/215 – Twilight over Parliament House in Canberra. Completed in 1988, the building's construction is estimated to have been the most expensive of any building in the world at the time.

215 left – The Great Southern tourist train crosses Boambee Creek, not far from Coffs Harbour.

215 right – The Brisbane skyline at sunset with the river of the same name in the foreground.

NEW ZEALAND
AUKLAND TO WELLINGTON

Departure: Auckland
Arrival: Wellington
Distance: 681 km (423 miles)
Duration: 10 hours 40 minutes
Stages: 7
Country: New Zealand

216/217 – The Northern Explorer tourist train crosses the daring Hapuawhenua Viaduct, now a tourist attraction in its own right, in Tongariro National Park.

Northern Explorer

In the heart of New Zealand, this tourist train from Auckland takes passengers to the capital of Wellington along a mountain railroad labeled an "engineering miracle."

The **Northern Explorer** is a tourist train that connects Auckland, the most populous city in New Zealand, with the capital city of Wellington three times a week, traveling north to south, or vice versa, across the North Island (one of the two main islands that make up this country in the South Pacific). Managed by Great Journeys of New Zealand, a division of the country's main railroad operator KiwiRail, it runs along 681 kilometers (423 miles) of the North Island Main Trunk, the main railroad line crossing the North Island.

Thanks to a smart, flexible ticket, it allows passengers to discover one of the most fascinating and scenic parts of New Zealand's territory. The train stops at seven stations between the two termini, and the ticket allows passengers to break up their route by stopping for a day or two in any of these locations before resuming the journey later on without hassle.

The Northern Explorer offers a quality service that targets the needs of tourist and pleasure travelers, but it is not a luxury train. So, there is an open car for admiring the landscape without a set of small windows, but there are no dining cars with crystal glassware, nor a saloon car with piano. The formula adopted by the Northern Explorer has been very successful, and that success continues to grow each year. This is thanks in part to the ride itself, which, potential extra stops aside, is made during the day and lasts about twelve hours.

A few words should be said about the railroad that the train travels, which has been described as an **"engineering miracle"** by industry experts. The route certainly is especially uneven and difficult due to the

217 – The Kapiti Coast seen from the viewpoint of a Northern Explorer coach.

218 – A panoramic overview of the city of Auckland from the bay at Stanley Point.

mountainous territory it navigates.

The railroad adopts what is known as a **"cape gauge,"** with a breadth of 1,067 millimeters (3.5 feet). It is also a mostly single-track route, with frequent crossings and passing sidings. About 65% of the line (460 kilometers, about 285 miles) is electrified, with two different power systems, at 1600 V DC and 25 kV AC. The line was built in functional sections, and the first to become operational was opened in 1873 from Auckland to the south, while the works began from Wellington only in 1885. It was completed in 1908 and the following year was fully operational.

The first trains, then with steam traction, took about twenty hours to complete the journey, and today the time required has been essentially cut in half.

The North Island Main Trunk required the construction of 352 bridges (on 681 kilometers/423 miles of line!) and fourteen tunnels, in addition to using certain engineering expedients, including the famous Raurimu Spiral, where **the track makes a complete turn**, bringing it to a significantly higher altitude above the point where the curve started,

overcoming a height difference of 139 meters (456 feet).

This set of engineering works makes the route a fantastic vehicle for discovering the North Island's lush interior, and the Northern Explorer makes the experience easy and enjoyable for everyone.

The train spends three days a week heading south and three days heading north: from Auckland to Wellington on Mondays, Thursdays, and Saturdays, and Wellington to Auckland on Wednesdays, Fridays, and Sundays. It stops at the following seven stations, from north to south: Papakura, Hamilton Frankton, Otorohanga, National Park, Ohakune, Palmerston North, and Paraparaumu.

The Northern Explorer coaches offer one level of service. All seats are the same, and the only choice offered is according to their arrangement in the carriages, either side-by-side seats facing the train's direction of travel (which are rotated before each journey) or at a table seating four people, ideal for groups and families. The large, spacious carriages have large windows, which even cover part of the ceiling. The train includes a bar and lounge carriage as well as an open, panoramic carriage, allowing passengers to become even

219 top – A nice shot of the Waikato River Bridge in Hamilton, one of the cities on the Northern Explorer itinerary.

219 bottom – The Emerald Lakes in Tongariro National Park, reachable via the Northern Explorer.

220 top – The beautiful New Zealand landscape, with the canyons around the Rangitikei River.

220 bottom – Palmerston North's main square, with its clock tower.

further acquainted with the surrounding landscape.

One service included in the ticket is an audio guide accessible via the arm of the passenger seat, for which a headset is provided during the trip. The audio commentary offers a constant flow of history, stories, and facts about the surrounding scenery, told in time with the train as it passes by. One very important opportunity the Northern Explorer provides is the option to **split one's itinerary** into several stages using the same ticket, with no price increase. Passengers can stop at select stations and board again free of charge at a later time, provided that they have notified the ticketing and reservations service more than three days in advance of the trip.

The Northern Explorer departs from Auckland Strand station, crossing the outskirts of the city, and immerses itself in an area where agricultural lands alternate with industrial warehouses. The train skirts the Waikato River and passes by Mount Taupiri (287 meters, about 942 feet), the **sacred mountain** of the Waikato people. Hamilton is the first major stop on the train. Following this city, the landscape starts to become more interesting, and travelers can appreciate how green and lush New Zealand is. The train passes through Te Kuiti, and on the left, immediately following the station, passengers can see a statue depicting a man shearing a sheep, as Te Kuiti is considered the sheep shearing capital of the world. A few minutes later, the Northern Explorer travels along the Waiteti Viaduct, built in 1887 and the oldest viaduct on the North Island Main Trunk Railway. The train follows the picturesque Ongarue River to Taumarunui, past which it comes upon the famous **Raurimu Spiral**, nestled in the dense rainforest. Immediately after coming through the top of the spiral, the train stops at the Tongariro National Park station, where the volcanic mountains can be seen

INTERESTING FACTS

The stops along the Northern Explorer route easily allow passengers to see much more on their journey. Among the most popular stops is Otorohanga, for the magical Waitomo Caves, a huge complex of limestone caves inhabited by millions of luminescent glowworms, insects similar to fireflies, which create the impression of a starry sky. The National Park station is the access point for the Tongariro Alpine Crossing, a 19-kilometer (about 12-mile) trek that can be covered in eight hours and is very popular on the Volcanic Plateau. Ohakune, on the other hand, is renowned for its winter skiing but is also quickly becoming a popular stop for its off-road cycling routes, especially the Old Coach Road.

in the distance. The train, having left the National Park, faces a series of impressive viaducts set within a dense thicket, overlooking deep gorges with streams running through them. After stopping for about half an hour in Ohakune, the train crosses the Tangiwai Bridge, then tackles the famous Turangarere horseshoe curve, which is essentially **a giant hairpin turn**, making a 180-degree bend, on the side of a valley. From here, the line begins to follow the astonishing Rangitikei River gorge, traveling over a series of large viaducts. The Northern Explorer begins to descend from the Volcanic Plateau to Marton, then stops at Feilding (which holds the title of **New Zealand's Most Beautiful Town**) and then reaches Palmerston North, where, until 1963, the railway cut across the town's main square. The train now follows a very scenic stretch of coast, and, as dusk approaches, it nears the impressive Wellington station, inaugurated in 1937 and set at the very heart of the city, not far from New Zealand's Parliament.

Of course, a stop at each of the seven intermediate stations will allow travelers to discover many other beautiful and intriguing sights surrounding this train and the main railroad line.

221 left – The site of the Tangiwai disaster. On the night of December 24, 1953, a bridge collapse caused a derailment, with 151 deaths.

221 top right – The iconic clock tower in Feilding, a location that has won the annual title of New Zealand's Most Beautiful Town fifteen times.

221 bottom right – The monumental entrance to Wellington station, inaugurated in 1937, and a terminal station of the Northern Explorer.

Photo Credits

All the maps are by GIULIA LOMBARDO.

Shutterstock.com pages:

1, 3, 4–5, 7, 9, 12, 19 all, 20 top, center and bottom, 23, 25 bottom, 26, 27 top, 28–29 all, 32, 34 bottom, 35, 36–37 all, 39 center and bottom, 43 all, 44, 46, 47 top and bottom right, 48–49, 50–51 all, 52–53 all, 54–55 all, 58–59, 60–61 all, 62 all, 66 bottom, 67, 70, 71 center and bottom, 74, 77 all, 81 bottom left and right, 82–83 all, 84, 85 bottom, 91, 92–93 all, 94–95 all, 96 bottom, 100–101 all, 102–103 all, 104, 106–107 all, 108–109 all, 112 top and bottom, 113, 114–115 all, 116, 118 bottom, 121, 123, 127 top and center, 128 top, 131, 132, 133 top and bottom left, 136–137 all, 138–139 all, 142–143 all, 144–145, 147 top right and left, 148–149, 150–151, 152, 154–155 all, 165, 166–167 all, 168, 169 top, 170 bottom, 171, 172–173, 175 all, 176–177 all, 178–179 all, 180–181 all, 183, 184, 186–187 all, 188–189, 188 bottom right, 190–191 all, 192–193 all, 194–195 all, 198 bottom, 199 right, 203 left, 207 left, 208 all, 209 top, 212 all, 213 top, 214–215, 215 bottom right, 218–219 all, 220–221 all.

Pages 6, 8: Courtesy of the Alaska Railroad Corporation

Pages 10–11 all, 13 all, 14–15 all: Courtesy of the Rocky Mountaineer

Pages 16–17, 18, 20–21: Courtesy of Via Rail Canada

Page 17: Robert McGouey/Industry/Alamy Stock Photo

Pages 22–23, 24: Courtesy of Amtrak/Joel Hawthorn

Page 25 top: Pete van der Spek/Alamy Stock Photo

Page 27 bottom: Ian Dagnall/Alamy Stock Photo

Page 30: Archivart/Alamy Stock Photo

Pages 30–31: Courtesy of Amtrak/Mike Danneman

Page 33: Auk Archive/Alamy Stock Photo

Pages 34–35: Nick Suydam/Alamy Stock Photo

Page 38: H. Mark Weidman Photography/Alamy Stock Photo

Page 39 top: Damon Shaw/Alamy Stock Photo

Page 40: Zoonar GmbH/Alamy Stock Photo

Page 41: Pat & Chuck Blackley/Alamy Stock Photo

Page 42: Zoonar GmbH/Alamy Stock Photo

Page 45: Horizon Images/Motion/Alamy Stock Photo

Page 47 left: Arterra/Getty Images

Page 48: Prisma by Dukas Presseagentur GmbH/Alamy Stock Photo

Pages 56–57, 57: imageBROKER/Alamy Stock Photo

Page 63: Retro AdArchives/Alamy Stock Photo

Pages 64 top, 65 all, 66–67: Courtesy of the Belmond

Page 64 bottom: Wolfgang Kaehler/LightRocket/Getty Images Management Limited/Martin Scott Powell/Matt Hind/David Noton

Page 68: Marius Dobilas/Alamy Stock Photo

Pages 68–69: Courtesy of the Norges beste AS

Page 71 top: Andrey Armyagov/Alamy Stock Photo

Pages 72–73: canbedone/Alamy Stock Photo

Page 73 top: Courtesy of the Vy/Øivind Haug

Page 73 bottom: Nataliya Nazarova/Alamy Stock Photo

Pages 74–75, 76: Colouria Media/Alamy Stock Photo

Pages 78–79 all, 80: Courtesy of the Belmond Management Limited/ Paul Blowfield/Matt Crossick

Page 81 top: Lee Thomas/Alamy Stock Photo

Pages 84–85, 86–87: Phil Metcalfe/Alamy Stock Photo

Pages 88–89: John Carroll Photography/Alamy Stock Photo

Pages 90–91: Klaus-Dietmar Gabbert/Getty Images

Pages 96–97 top: picture alliance/Getty Images

Page 97 bottom: picture alliance/Getty Images

Pages 98–99: McPhoto/Rolfes/Alamy Stock Photo

Pages 110, 110–111: VW Pics/Getty Images

Page 112 center: Loop Images Ltd/Alamy Stock Photo

Pages 116–117: Alexandre Roussel/Alamy Stock Photo

Page 118 top: Roussel Bernard/Alamy Stock Photo

Page 119: Martin Thomas Photography/Alamy Stock Photo

Pages 120–121, 122: Didier Zylberyng/Alamy Stock Photo

Page 124: Digitalman/Alamy Stock Photo

Pages 124–125: Christophe Boisvieux/Alamy Stock Photo

Page 126: Jon Arnold Images Ltd/Alamy Stock Photo

Page 127 bottom: Hemis/Alamy Stock Photo

Page 128 bottom: Jon Ingall/Alamy Stock Photo

Page 129: Pascal Pochard-Casabianca/Getty Images

Pages 130–131: Realy Easy Star/Alamy Stock Photo

Page 133 right: jbdodane/Alamy Stock Photo

Page 134: Courtesy of Franco Tanel

Pages 140–141 all: Courtesy of the Belmond Management Limited/

   Paul Blowfield/Matt Crossick

Page 144: RZAF_Images/Alamy Stock Photo

Page 146: Yasuyoshi Chiba/Getty Images

Page 147 bottom: dpa picture alliance/Alamy Stock Photo

Page 148: rosinka/Stockimo/Alamy Stock Photo

Pages 152–153: imageBROKER/Alamy Stock Photo

Pages 156–157 all, 158–159 all, 160–161 all, 162–163 all: Courtesy of

   Rovos Rail Tours

Pages 164–165, 169 bottom: mauritius images GmbH/Alamy Stock

   Photo

Page 170: Dmitrii Rud/Alamy Stock Photo

Page 172: Courtesy of the Royal Indian Trains

Page 173 bottom: IndiaPicture/Alamy Stock Photo

Page 174 top and bottom: Courtesy of the Royal Indian Trains

Page 182: Design Pics Inc/Alamy Stock Photo

Pages 184–185: Imaginechina Limited/Alamy Stock Photo

Page 188 bottom left: China Photos/Getty Images

Page 196 top: catwalkphotos/Alamy Stock Photo

Pages 196 bottom, 196–197, 198 top: Courtesy of the Belmond

   Management Limited/Matt Hind/Ian Lloyd/Ron Bambridge

Page 199 left: Jeremy Horner/Alamy Stock Photo

Page 200: Kyodo News/Getty Images

Pages 201, 202, 203 right: Tomohiro Ohsumi/Getty Images

Pages 204–205 all, 206: Courtesy of the Journey Beyond

Pages 207 right, 209 bottom: Lisa Maree Williams/Getty Images

Pages 210–211 all, 215 bottom left: Courtesy of the Journey Beyond

Page 213 bottom: Jon Arnold Images Ltd /Alamy Stock Photo

Pages 216–217 all: Courtesy of the Great Journeys of New Zealand/

   KiwiRail/Alan O'Brien/Robin Heyworth

Cover

Shutterstock

Back cover

Background: Vector Tradition/Shutterstock

left: marlys grisson/Shutterstock

right: Courtesy of the Journey Beyond

About the Author

FRANCO TANEL is a journalist and photographer who began his professional career in 1979 working with the photographic agency D-Day. He has since collaborated with several major Italian photojournalism agencies, including Contrasto and Grazia Neri. Tanel focuses especially on topics related to transportation and infrastructure, including sustainable tourism and the environment, as well as issues related to immigration, always combining his journalistic and photography work. For many years, he covered transport and urban planning in specialist periodicals for the Italian newspaper *Il Sole 24 Ore* and has collaborated with *Tuttotreno*, Italy's foremost periodical dedicated to rail travel, since its inception. He was part of the working group that founded the Green Logistics Expo, the first Italian fair dedicated to transport and sustainable logistics.

Project editor VALERIA MANFERTO DE FABIANIS
Editorial assistant GIORGIO FERRERO
Graphic design MARIA CUCCHI

Shelter Harbor Press

603 W. 115th Street, Suite 163
New York, NY 10025
www.shelterharborpress.com

This edition published by Shelter Harbor Press by arrangement with White Star s.r.l.

Cataloging-in-Publication Data has been applied for and may be obtained from the Library of Congress.

ISBN: 978-1-62795-191-3

For sales please contact info@shelterharborpress.com

10 9 8 7 6 5 4 3 2 1

WS White Star Publishers® is a registered trademark property of White Star s.r.l.

© 2023 White Star s.r.l.
Piazzale Luigi Cadorna, 6
20123 Milan, Italy
www.whitestar.it

Translator: Megan Bredeson
Editor: Abby Young

This book is published by White Star Publishers in the United Kingdom. The title in the UK is **Travel by Train!**
ISBN: 978-8-85441-977-3

Printed in China